Valerie Roman is an impressive leader: collaborative, knowledgeable, and deeply in touch with the needs of employees and clients. Striving for a better future, Valerie embraces both teamwork and leadership that is both inspiring and instructive. Hat Trick shows not only how she juggled many responsibilities efficiently, but shows her wise ways of living and working.

– *Maya Townsend, Organization Development Consultant, Partnering Resources*

I0224546

What people are saying about Valerie Roman's *Hat Trick*:

Finally! A book that not only acknowledges how difficult it can be for women to achieve a work/life balance, but also offers practical tools to get there. As a freelance theater director/choreographer, mother to a toddler, and wife to a man with a very demanding full-time job, I am constantly trying to find ways to minimize stress and find joy in the daily grind. Hat Trick will be my new and much-needed guide.
  – *Jen Wineman, Director/Choreographer*

Growing up, if my mother didn't know the answer to my problem, she would meticulously research it until she had seven possible solutions in a labeled binder. In *Hat Trick*, she shares her lessons learned and research over four decades that will help you every day. After all, that is what her life has always been about — not just learning something for herself, but spreading it around for others to know as well. However, I'm still the only one who can text her from the bar on Trivia Nights to learn Eddie Johnston was the backup goalie for the 1970 Stanley Cup Champion Boston Bruins. That gets me free food and beer for the table, and I'm not giving that up.
  – *David Roman, Mental Health Clinician*

Balance is such an important component in living a meaningful life. In Hat Trick, Valerie Roman chronicles what she has learned—both through trial and error and through research—about building a successful career and leading a fulfilling life. I will happily offer this to my thirty-year-old daughter as she crafts her life as a wife, mother, entrepreneur, and friend, and who will undoubtedly profit from Valerie's wit and wisdom, as I have.
  – *Anne Ferguson, Director of College Counseling*
    Phillips Academy and Hathaway Brown School

Hat Trick provides solid tips on practical living for women of all ages about balancing their own needs with their many obligations. We can all relate to Valerie Roman's personal experiences woven into her generous advice that she cultivated from a variety of reliable sources. This is a book that will have a permanent place on my bookshelf and one that I will share with my daughter.
  – *Elaine Crivelli, Faculty Emerita, Phillips Academy*

Now that I've grown to realize how difficult it is to manage both a professional and personal life, I have a much greater appreciation for my mom. Always an amazing mother to my brother and me, she didn't bring her work home. Still, she navigated a path to the top in the tough, male-dominated field of information technology while always making me feel that being my mom was her most important job. She's always found a way to help me whenever I needed it. Now that I have read Hat Trick, I'm confident she'll be able to help you, too.
  – *Matt Roman, Television Writer*

Sensitive to the insecurities of recent graduates, Hat Trick is a playbook for a young woman who is moving into the major leagues. With humor and true helpfulness, author Valerie Roman shows how to score your goals without losing your balance.
  – *Alexa Zannetos, Senior Wall Street Attorney*

As a young woman navigating the hurdles of combining a successful career with a good personal life, I learned much from working with Valerie Roman during a political campaign. Hat Trick is an empowering collection of Valerie Roman's tried-and-true recommendations that any woman would benefit from. If you aren't lucky enough to have Valerie Roman as a friend, mom, or colleague, Hat Trick is the next-best thing.
  – *Britt Edwards, Political Strategist*

As an architect with a special interest in urban design, and historic preservation, I welcome Valerie Roman's memoir, Hat Trick. Structuring a good life that includes family and friends, as well as professionalism and service, is a lot like designing a building from the ground up. To stand the test of time, you want it to be both beautiful and functional. This memoir includes private spaces as well as public ones, inspiring women to be true to themselves as they make their way along the long and wide road of opportunity that we women are fortunate to have in the 21st century. Inspiring and informative, Valerie Roman is a trusted guide.
  – *Anne Reilly Fahim, Architect, AFASPC*

As a champion of women in the workplace, I applaud Valerie Roman for finding her own success and for sharing her tips with others. Role models in any sphere are important, and Valerie Roman, who has scored a hat trick in her own life with family, career and service, is a great role model for women starting out. Her book will coach you through difficult situations, everyday anxieties, and exciting opportunities at work and at home.
  – *Joy Ohm, Advocate for Women in the Workplace*

The image of a three-goal hat trick aptly describes Valerie Roman's accomplishments. First, she has developed a positive sense of self, while becoming a role model for others. Secondly, she has had a successful and fulfilling career in the technology field; and thirdly, she has nurtured loving, caring relationships with her family and friends. This hat trick will inspire readers of her book to achieve a hat trick of their own.
  – *Sheila Segal, Teacher*

HAT TRICK

HAT TRICK

THE ESSENTIAL PLAYBOOK FOR
CAREER, FAMILY, AND PERSONAL BALANCE

By Valerie Roman

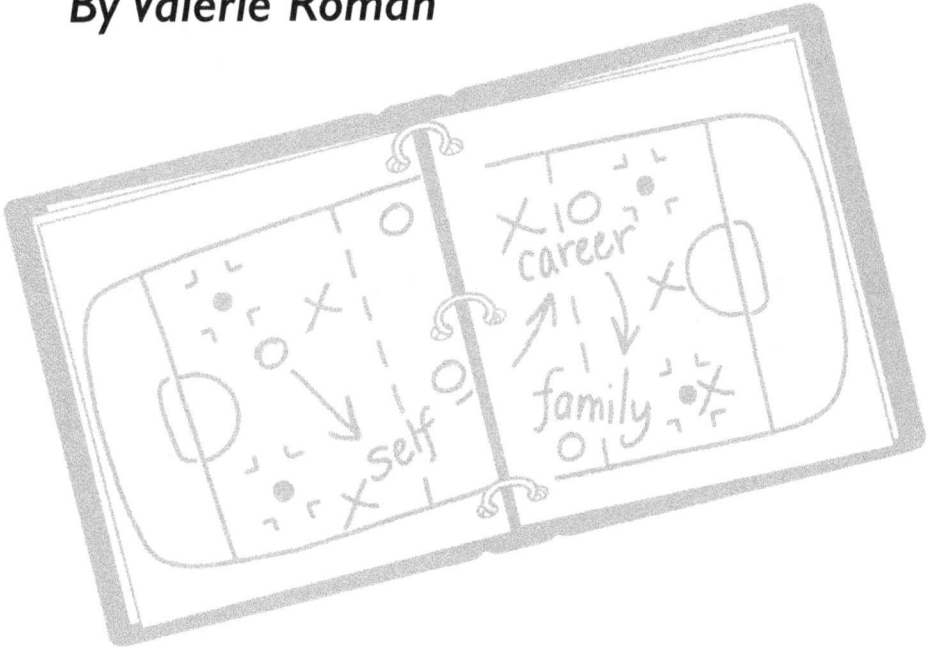

DPWN Publishing • West Chicago, IL 60185

Printed in the United States of America.

Published by DPWN Publishing. For permission to reprint from the book in any form, please contact HatTrickPlaybook@gmail.com.

Library of Congress Control Number: 2018914793

ISBN: 978-1-939794-17-8 paperback
ISBN: 978-0-692-17787-7 hardcover

Roman, Valerie
Hat Trick: The Essential Playbook for Career, Family, and Personal Balance
    Includes internet resources and bibliographical references
    1. Women-psychology 2. Self-realization
    646 BIO022000

Book Design by Holly Harper, Blue Bike Communications

Illustrations by Hannah Dautel, HD Illustration

hat trick

noun

Definition.

1
: the scoring of three goals in one game (as in hockey or soccer) by a single player

2
: a series of three victories, successes, or related accomplishments

To my mother for providing the model of a wife and mother, and to my father for teaching me the love of sports and its importance in our lives.

Foreword

When I am asked how I managed to run a multi-million-dollar organization while I raised a family, traveled the world, and still had time for vacations at the shore, I don't know where to begin. In many ways, we women of the seventies and eighties were still pioneers in our climb to the top. We did many things well, but on an ad hoc basis. We never had time to sit down and analyze the new way of life women were establishing in America. In too many cases, we left balance out of the equation. Happily, my friend Valerie Roman, never one to leave anything to chance, researched and saved all the advice she could find—from magazines, books, and websites over forty years—to compile a roadmap to success in every aspect of a woman's life.

I was thrilled that Valerie Roman's compilation of strategies and shortcuts for the working woman would soon be available in this new book. She has captured the key issues that women face as we work to balance it all—career, family, and personal well-being—and has provided a helpful guide to navigate the myriad of issues we confront day to day.

Valerie Roman was first friends with my husband, as they started their careers at the U.S. Census Bureau and shared their love of sports. It wasn't long before she became my go-to girlfriend for endless laughs, thoughtful advice, and the always-available shoulder to lean on. We have been friends for forty years now, and in all those years, of all the women I have known, without hesitation I can think of no one better than Valerie Roman to write such a book. I recommend this book to any woman who wants to live life to its fullest.

Valerie Roman is an uber sports fan. When I learned that she had titled her book *Hat Trick*, it made perfect sense. In hockey, when a player scores three goals in a single game—no easy feat—it is called a hat trick, and fans honor the player by throwing their hats onto the ice. Valerie Roman has accomplished her own hat trick in life, making it as a respected technology trailblazer in a male-dominated field, a happy wife of 35 years and mother of two successful children, and a treasured friend and supporter to many people and causes—a genuine example of a balanced woman.

In this book, Valerie Roman shares her common-sense approach to success at every stage of life. She first pinpoints goals, and then researches how to attain them. She does not prioritize or plan until she is sure of all the possibilities. In *Hat Trick*, she's done the homework for us.

With decades of research from many sources, Valerie Roman presents tips in this easy-to-use guide, figuring that if they helped her, they will help others. She has tips on everything from dealing with holiday celebrations such as the dreaded cookie exchange, to departmental meetings and preparation of the agenda for success, as well as finding the right wellness program that meets your needs. Easy-to-access topics, from nutrition and career development to marriage and relationships, are covered in this comprehensive collection for the woman who wants balance in every aspect of her life.

I welcome Valerie Roman's *Hat Trick* to my library, both as a memoir and as a handy reference. It is a hard-copy Internet search almanac with heart and humor, a compendium of truly useful information for a balanced life well lived. You will get a whole new take on lifelong learning no matter your age. Valerie Roman takes you on her journey so that you, your daughters, and friends can benefit from her experiences. Her valuable tips will save you time and guide your way. I know you will benefit from her expertise, just as I have had the privilege of doing for so many decades. Her playbook never disappoints.

Hat Trick is worth your time! Enjoy!

Kathryn Kretschmer-Weyland, Chief Operating Officer
U.S. Mayor Enterprises, Inc.
Silver Spring, Maryland

Contents

LET THE GAME BEGIN   *1*

GOAL ONE: **TAKE CARE OF YOURSELF**   *11*

Chapter 1	Weight Watching	*19*
Chapter 2	Getting and Staying Fit	*31*
Chapter 3	Energy Boosts	*39*
Chapter 4	Looking Good	*45*
Chapter 5	Health and Wellness	*55*
Chapter 6	Improve Your Memory	*77*
Chapter 7	The Hunt for Happiness	*85*

GOAL TWO: **HAVE A GREAT CAREER**   *99*

Chapter 8	Women and the Workplace	*103*
Chapter 9	Skills for Success	*121*
Chapter 10	Handling Stress	*129*
Chapter 11	Saving Time	*141*
Chapter 12	Organizing the Office	*151*

GOAL THREE: **RAISE A HAPPY FAMILY**   *159*

Chapter 13	Marriage and Relationships	*169*
Chapter 14	Organizing the Home	*179*
Chapter 15	Parenting Pointers	*187*
Chapter 16	The Cooking Conundrum	*205*
Chapter 17	Cleaning Tips	*211*
Chapter 18	Conquering the Clutter	*219*

SAVOR THE VICTORY   *227*

ACKNOWLEDGEMENTS   *233*
RESOURCES   *235*
INDEX   *239*
ABOUT THE AUTHOR   *243*

Let the Game Begin

Because I had only one sibling—a sister who was eight years older—I believe my dad may have wanted me to be a boy. He was a huge Boston sports fan and began to take me to games when I was very young. We also talked a lot about sports and watched them on television together. We went to Boston (now New England) Patriots games back in the "bad times" when the team did not win, and we would see the Bruins and the Celtics—locally known as the B's and the C's—at the old Boston Garden. I cried over their losses and jumped up and down at their wins. And I always believed that where I sat and what I wore had a direct effect on my team's performance and the game's outcome.

Since then, watching sports has always been an important part of my life. On his deathbed, my dad reminded me of how proud he was of me and then demonstrated the depth of his love when he said, "Honey, I hope you get to see a Red Sox championship during your lifetime, since I obviously did not get to see one during mine." Sports bonded us to the very end.

From sharing sports with my father, I learned many life lessons. I came to admire teamwork and to understand why sportsmanship is so central to the game. I remained faithful to

1

my teams through their losing streaks and celebrated fully when they were on top. I learned to appreciate the accomplishment of a difficult task, as I demonstrated when I tossed my hat onto the ice after a hockey player scored three goals, known as a hat trick. The utter joy of recognizing a game well played has stayed with me throughout my lifetime, thanks to my father.

> *Many women do not follow sports much, but all participate in another game—the pursuit of perfection.*

Many women do not follow sports much, but all participate in another game—the pursuit of perfection. Beginning at a young age, girls are provided with various prototypes of the perfect woman—a Barbie doll, a television or movie star, a famous doctor, a world-renowned athlete, or a supermodel. As they grow older, girls continue to confront unrealistic ideals of who they are supposed to be and what they are supposed to do to be successful. The image of the perfect woman may have changed over time, but its existence has remained constant.

In the 1950s and early 1960s, not many real-life role models were available to girls. It was not that such role models did not exist—it was just not easy to learn about these women. Girls like me were exposed to such seemingly unattainable roles as those of movie stars Audrey Hepburn and Grace Kelly. And we watched housewives in television shows, such as *Leave It to Beaver, Father Knows Best,* and *The Donna Reed Show.* These were happy women whose career goals were getting their kids off to school and their husbands off to work, keeping the house clean, and serving dinner on time.

Thankfully, as a by-product of the women's movement, the professional woman as a role model was introduced in the late 1960s and early 1970s in television shows about women in career positions. In *Julia,* Diahann Carroll played the first nonstereotypical network television role for an African-American woman as Julia Baker, a single mom who worked full time as a nurse. In *The Mary Tyler Moore Show*, Moore portrayed Mary Richards, a career-oriented single woman who moved alone to Minneapolis to become a television station news producer. The doors were opening for women to succeed in a traditionally male-dominated workforce.

The 1970s introduced the "superwoman," strong and beautiful with both a high-powered career and a family, such as actresses Jane Fonda and Candace Bergen. The 1980s brought us actresses Meryl Streep and Sigourney Weaver; the 1990s, Olympic soccer champion Mia Hamm and actress Sandra Bullock. In the 21st century, we have seen actress and businesswoman Jessica Alba and former First Lady and lawyer Michelle Obama stand out as gorgeous and professionally accomplished, while caring not only for their own children but also for children everywhere. Recently, we have been introduced to the beautifully turned-out CEOs with lovely families: Sheryl Sandberg of Facebook, Meg Whitman of Hewlett Packard, and Indra Nooyi of PepsiCo. While the emphasis on which achievements count the most may vary from decade to decade, the expectation that a woman will excel as a personality in her own right, as a leader in her field, and as a successful wife and mother keeps women training for perfection throughout their lives.

> *"Superwoman" —strong and beautiful with both a high-powered career and a family.*

I began to play this game when I left my small town of Somersworth, New Hampshire, to attend college. Ironically, despite my love for men's sports, I attended Wellesley College, a prestigious women's school with no men's sports teams to follow. However, I was urged there to strive for excellence, be a leader, and make a difference in the world. Wellesley instilled in me the goal to be the best and to seek perfection. There I began the journey to accomplish my own personal three-goal hat trick:

1. Take care of myself, and live a long, healthy, and fulfilling life that produces the best "me" I can be;
2. Have a great career that is successful and satisfying;
3. Raise a happy family and be the best wife and mother I can be.

Feeling the need to learn so much more to accomplish my goals, I decided to start my research as a sophomore. I took an empty hatbox from my mother's closet and began to stuff it with the best articles I could find for becoming the successful, fulfilled person I wanted to be. I began to fill the hatbox with magazine and newspaper articles on topics ranging from eating sufficient fiber in my diet, organizing closets, and asking my boss for a raise. My mother, a suburban housewife, could not teach me all I needed to know to become a successful "Do It All" woman. I had to learn that on my own from what I read, and it worked. As the contents of the hatbox grew, so did my belief that I could succeed and score my own hat trick.

When my mother married my father in 1947, she brought a chest filled with beautiful linens and lace to their first home. Called a hope chest, this was standard for the American bride at the time—a place where young women kept embroidered linens and knitted blankets for their homes after marriage. My mom's hope chest, about the size of a bed for a large golden retriever, rested against a wall in my parents' bedroom. It was made of solid, dark mahogany. Each week my mother polished it, and a fresh lemon scent filled the room. She placed a white doily, embroidered by my grandmother, on the center of it, anchored with a vase of flowers. I smelled the sweet scent of its cedar lining every time I opened it.

When I married 35 years later, I brought the hatbox to my new home. It did not smell as nice as my mother's hope chest, but it did contain information on how I could become the most organized, content, loved, and successful woman, wife, mother, friend, and professional I could be. While my mother's chest contained beautifully hand-tatted tablecloths and bed linens, mine contained articles with titles like "25 Ways to Deal with an Incompetent Boss" and "Best Dinners You Can Make and Eat in 14 Minutes."

As my life progressed through a career, marriage, and raising children, I continued to add articles to the hatbox, as well as my own written notes of what I had learned along the way. My collection expanded into bigger and bigger boxes.

When my children grew up and I retired from my job, I had less need for the advice in the hatbox. But somehow I could never part with this treasure chest of tips and lessons. I thought that since it had helped me so much, maybe it could help other women. After all, it was a sifted assembly of great advice from so many magazines and newspapers—*Better Homes & Gardens, Eating Well, Family Circle, Family Fun, First for Women, Glamour, Good Housekeeping, Ladies' Home Journal,* the *New York Times,* O the *Oprah Magazine, Parenting, Prevention, Professional Woman's Magazine, Psychology Today, Real Simple, Redbook, USA Today, Vogue, Woman's Day, Women's Health, Working Mother*—as well as books, websites, and television shows, such as *The Doctors* and *The Dr. Oz Show.* Many of the pearls of wisdom I had kept saved me from the various perils of life, ranging from wearing the wrong earrings for my facial structure, to not getting enough vitamins in my diet, to hiring a loser for a job.

Since the articles in the hatbox had taught me to be organized, I sat down and typed up the information I had collected from them. Some advice I had to disregard, because it was out of date. I smiled over the recommendations to create the "big hair" look, I shook my head over the advice about now unsafe children's car seats, and I read aloud the articles on office etiquette in the 1980s to my chortling husband. Times do change. Nobody questioned the environmental impact of disposable diapers in the 1980s. Dressing in stilettos was considered good business practice in the 1990s, because it allegedly impressed the customers. Women competing with other women at the end of the century was considered the best way to get ahead. Nonetheless, much of the other information I had collected still remained useful in building a better life.

Life for the modern woman is a juggling act. Most of the materials I have read on ways to maintain a marriage, manage a household with children, and advance along one's chosen career track have been prescriptive, based on such famous role models as lifestylist Martha Stewart at home and philanthropist Judith Rodin in the workplace. However, I have learned that it is unrealistic to adhere to a preconceived notion of what the modern woman should achieve. Each of us should set our own life goals based on our abilities, needs, and dreams.

I do not buy into the role model way of doing things. In fact, I am the antidote for women who have been deluded by famous role models. I am but a sports fan from New Hampshire who does not cook, yet who tenaciously has found ways to stay healthy and happy while balancing a fulfilling career with great friends and a wonderful family. I am not a role model—I just want to share what I know and what I have learned.

I just want to share what I know and what I have learned.

The magazine articles and the notes from self-help books that I gathered and saved in the hatbox offer practical, focused solutions to life's little annoyances and mysteries, unattached to any celebrity or star. I want to share the secrets and tips that have worked for me with hope that they will work for other women, as well. I am sharing them in this single, handy volume you now hold in your hands, which I hope will do for you what Isabella Beeton's *Mrs. Beeton's Book of Household Management* did for Victorian women and Shirley Conran's *Superwoman: Everywoman's Book of Household Management* did for the London swingers of the 1970s. I realized a while back that, while I am neither famous nor a role model, I am fulfilled. I have good health; have had a loving marriage for over 30 years; have had a successful career; and have raised two admirable young men who are now starting their own careers.

Throughout my 35 years of moving up the career ladder, finding happiness with my husband and children, and enjoying life to its fullest, I have collected useful advice that may be valuable to others. I offer to you my lifetime of lessons, my stockpile of struggles and successes, and my years of relentless research on an array of topics. I hope this book will help you on the challenging, but always fascinating, journey to score your own hat trick in life, whatever that may be—and to become the best version of yourself that you possibly can.

GOAL ONE
TAKE CARE OF YOURSELF

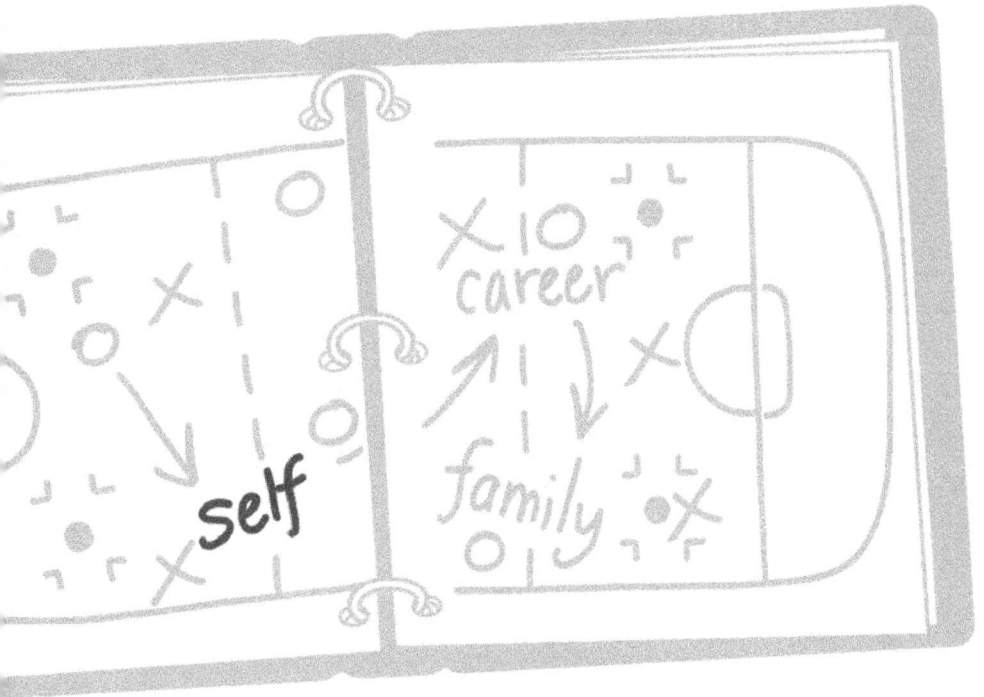

Goal One
Take Care of Yourself

I was born in 1956—a baby boomer—and grew up in Somersworth, a small town in New Hampshire. My dad, George Anthonakes, worked for General Electric, its main employer. My mom, Esther Anthonakes, was a housewife. I had one older sister, Pam, and a dog named Cookie. It was our version of Thornton Wilder's *Our Town*.

My dad was a 1950s sort of guy, like Ozzie Nelson in the TV show *The Adventures of Ozzie and Harriet*. He provided for our family and always had our safety and well-being foremost in his mind. He had always wanted to go to college, but as the oldest child growing up, he needed to work to financially support his family. He never resented that role, yet he felt the lack of a college education was a barrier to his income potential. He worked as an electrical engineer, but since he did not have a degree, he earned less than the engineering degree holders did. He frequently reminded us of that fact. Dad was determined not to allow financial uncertainty in the lives of his children. He had three dreams for us: He wanted each of his daughters to go to college, have a good job, and walk down the aisle on his arm to happy and holy matrimony.

As I was growing up, my mother truly was the model

housewife of the 1950s. Her children and husband came before she did. Everyone's clothes were impeccably cleaned, bleached, and ironed. My father left for work each day with a lunch in hand, packed by my mother. She greeted my sister and me after school with milk and cookies. And she placed a hot meal on the table within 30 minutes of Dad's arriving home from a hard day at work. Mom was good at her roles of wife and mother.

This was remarkable when you consider the childhood my mother had. When my mom was five years old, her mother died while giving birth to a son. Her infant brother was taken in by close relatives, but my mother was bounced around to live in various relatives' houses, while her father ran his candy-making store in Boston. When my grandfather remarried, his new younger wife physically and psychologically abused my mother. She would throw my mother's report card—all A's—down the stairs to the basement, and sometimes threw my mother down with it.

As she grew older, my mother dreamed of going to college. Relatives still tell me how smart she was and how much she deserved a college education. However, like my father, she was expected to help support her family. In contrast to my father, my mother always resented having to take on that responsibility. She worked full time as a file clerk until she met and married my father at the age of 21. When she had two daughters, she had dreams for us similar to those of our dad: college educations, careers, and big Greek weddings.

My family had moved from Massachusetts to New Hampshire when I was 4 and my sister was 12, so the move had much more of an impact on her than it did on me. Pam was angry with my father for uprooting her because of his job, frustrated with my mother for allowing it to happen, and resentful of me for adjusting more easily.

Many psychologists have written about first-child versus second-child behavior patterns, in which the older child is the more dutiful and the younger child is the more defiant. In our family, it was quite the opposite. My sister was the rebellious one, often testing my parents to see exactly how far she could go. I was the "pleaser" child, the one who always wanted to do what was right and what would please my parents. Given the strength of my father's personality, my sister usually did not get very far, but frequently the test developed into a yelling session, in which my dad always had the last word. I would go upstairs to my bedroom, close the door, cuddle on my bed with my beagle, Cookie, and play the radio loudly enough to deafen the sounds from downstairs.

During Pam's high school years, the conversations at our dinner table frequently consisted of my parents encouraging her to prepare for and apply to college. However, whether out of defiance or personal choice, she emphatically said she had no interest in it.

In the evening after homework was finished, we would all sit in the den and watch television. We frequently watched *The Donna Reed Show* together, laughing at the particular family predicament of each episode and noting how Donna just seemed to solve all of her family's problems, all of the time. The show provided us with a prototype of the perfect woman. Donna was happy, calm, and beautifully dressed (including pearls). She was a college graduate and a former nurse. She cooked, baked, ironed, kept an impeccably clean and organized home, and constantly tended to the needs of her husband and children. Ironically, the daughter in the family, Mary, was just about the same age as my sister. I often noticed a look of envy on Pam's face as she watched Mary and Donna have heart-to-heart talks. Sometimes, I noticed a twinkle in my dad's eye as he watched Donna, with her beautiful figure, acting as the perfect wife to Dr. Alex Stone. My mother, in contrast, was overweight and later told me felt insecure about growing up both without a good mother for a role model and without a college education. She would witness Donna's apparent flawlessness, detect my family's reactions, and slowly leave the room looking dejected.

One day when I was seven years old, a psychologically traumatic event occurred in my family. My mother had finished cleaning up the dinner dishes and my dad had gone to a zoning board meeting. I was doing my homework at the kitchen table. Pam came downstairs and was planning to go out with friends. She wore a low cut, revealing shirt, a very short skirt, and high boots. I loudly blurted out, "Boy, Pam, you can almost see your boobies and bum."

"Why can't you be like Donna Reed? She's a great mother."

Pam yelled, "This is the style. Shut up, you stupid brat."

My mother quickly intervened and shouted, "Pam, you cannot go out in that outfit. You look horrible. Go up and change. Your father would have a fit if he saw you. And do not talk to your sister like that."

I am not sure why Pam then reacted the way she did. As she looked at my overweight mother in a Hawaiian muumuu, was she thinking about Donna Reed's chic belted dresses that accentuated her slim waistline? Was she thinking about how Donna never raised her voice? Did she wish our mom would be like Donna Reed and simply say to her daughter, "I trust you can choose a more appropriate outfit," instead of issuing commands? Was Pam thinking about how Donna confidently ran the household and made decisions, in contrast to my mother who let my father make the decision to leave our relatives and friends in Massachusetts and move to New Hampshire? I am not sure if it was one or all of those reasons, but as my sister ran back up the stairs, for the first time I heard her scream to my mother: "Why can't you be like Donna Reed? *She's* a great mother. Why can't you be like *her?!*"

My mother replied, "I am no Donna Reed! I am sorry! I never will be!"

I never forgot those words they exchanged. I thought of them throughout my childhood. Each time, I heard the defeated sound of my mother's voice and witnessed the sadness and look of failure on her face. From an early age, I became very aware of the perils of playing the game and experiencing what I call the Donna Reed Syndrome—trying to live up to some externally driven depiction of the perfect woman.

At the age of 19, my sister became pregnant and eloped. I vividly remember watching my father when he took her telephone call at the kitchen table, the same table where we had all shared so many conversations about goals and dreams. He was trying inconspicuously to wipe a tear off his cheek. I remember my mother pleading, "Please come home, Pam. We will fix everything, and you can have a real wedding." But Pam's call turned into a dial tone, and the wedding did not come to pass.

So, at the age of 11, I in effect became an only child. What was worse than losing a sister was that I became the only child who could make my parents' goals for both of us come true–a college education, a career, and a formal Greek wedding.

I carried that responsibility with me as I began my years at Wellesley, where I often wondered if I could succeed. After all, my college had graduated so many women of achievement–Secretary of State and Senator Hillary Clinton, news anchor Diane Sawyer, Secretary of State and U.N. Ambassador Madeleine Albright, and National Public Radio commentator Cokie Roberts, just to name a few. Many of my fellow students came from wealthy families and excellent boarding schools. Sure, I was high school valedictorian, but I came from a very small and not very highly rated public school. Nonetheless, my parents always encouraged me during those times at college when I just did not feel good enough. To reassure me, they would proudly recall our Greek heritage that was so important to our family. Since my father's family had emigrated from a village near Sparta and my mother's family had emigrated from Athens, my parents would say, "Val, you are blessed with the strength of Sparta and the wisdom of Athens. Do not ever let anyone make you feel less."

The fact is, I would not even have applied to Wellesley if it were not for my special high school teacher, Sheila Segal, who had graduated from there. Not many students from my school went away to college. They would go to the state university or not go at all. Our school's guidance counselor even forgot to notify us of the SAT test dates. However, Mrs. Segal saw something in me, brought me to visit her alma mater, and guided me through the college application process.

My college application process was not like it is today. I applied to only three schools: Simmons College in Boston, because my favorite cousin graduated from there, and it was within walking distance to Fenway Park, where my beloved Red Sox played; Wellesley College in Wellesley, Massachusetts, because Mrs. Segal had graduated from there, it had a beautiful campus, and it provided transportation to Boston, so I could get to Fenway Park; and the University of New Hampshire, since it seemed that every high school senior in New Hampshire applied there.

I used questionable reasoning in my selection process, to say the least. I was accepted to all three and originally thought I would attend Simmons College, because, of course, it was closest to Fenway Park. But in 1974, Boston was going through racial unrest and violent riots after the school busing rulings, and my father forbade me to live in that turmoil. So, I decided to go to Wellesley College. It is amazing to me how such a flawed decision-making process ended up with such a fabulous result: Wellesley was one of the best experiences of my life.

The transition from being a small-town girl from Somersworth, New Hampshire, to a Wellesley College student was not easy for me. Somersworth was a town where the majority of people were of French-Canadian descent. No Black, Latino, or Asian families were to be found. There were only two houses where Jewish people, the Cohens, lived, and they were related. Since my family was of Greek descent, the Cohens and we accounted for all of the town's ethnic diversity. In fact, soon after moving there, I remember hearing a woman at a supermarket ask another woman, "Did you hear that Greeks have moved into town?"

I was so naïve. I had grown up never being exposed to diversity or progressive thinking, and here I was in one of the most diverse and progressive educational institutions in the country. During the summer before I started, I was told my roommate would be a girl from Michigan named Clare. I had never met anyone from Michigan. We communicated over the summer about who would bring what for our dorm room. I discovered that she was only 4 feet, 11 inches tall, two inches shorter than I was. I thought we would have so much more in common and I was so excited. I had visions of the beginning of a lifelong relationship.

When I arrived, I found a room that was a single made into a double, with bookcases stacked on desks, one small closet, and a bunk bed. Clare had already moved her things in and left. My excitement about making joint decisions in how we would arrange our living space quickly turned into loneliness and fear. She had left very little room for me.

After a few hours, she walked in and said hello in an unwelcoming way. She announced that she was spending the night out with a friend who had traveled with her from Michigan and would be back the next day. So much for my pajama-party visions with my new roommate. I went to bed that night unable to hold back tears, wondering why I was there and fearful of what was to come.

The next day, Clare returned and said matter-of-factly, "My girlfriend will be spending the night here."

I immediately thought that this was the pajama party I was

17

expecting and replied, "That's great! The room is small, but we can all fit."

She looked at me and said, "No, you have it wrong. She is my *girlfriend*."

Again I responded, "Fine. I wish some of my girlfriends could have come for a visit, too."

She again looked at me in a strange way and said, "No, you will need to leave the room. She is my girlfriend, we are in love, and you cannot sleep here with us. You will need to find another place."

I finally understood that she was a lesbian. I was not bothered that she was a lesbian, but I was very bothered by her audacity to expect me to find somewhere else to sleep. However, I did not want to cause problems, so I agreed. I went down the hall to meet new people, hoping to find someone nice enough to let me sleep on her floor that night. Fortunately, I introduced myself to Cindy Romer, from Indiana, who lived right across the hall. When I told her of my predicament, I not only found a place to sleep for the night—I also began the lifelong relationship that I had envisioned. Cindy became one of my closest friends that second night on campus, and we are still close friends today.

I learned a great deal at Wellesley, both inside and outside the classroom. I discovered that things often work out for the best, even when they appear to be difficult. After all, if I had not been kicked out of my dorm room, I might have never met Cindy. If I had not been so challenged academically, sometimes to the point of thinking I could not cut it, I would not have learned the importance of perseverance, good study habits, and good health habits.

Chapter One
Weight Watching

I It was too far for my sophomore year college roommate, Andrea Mutch, to go home to South Dakota for Thanksgiving. Instead, she spent the holiday at my house, less than a two-hour drive from Wellesley. There she became fully acquainted with our Greek love of large quantities of food. We would eat from the moment we arrived to the moment we left. We ate Greek delicacies, such as dolmades, pastitsio, and baklava. We ate non-Greek delicacies, such as potato chips, Oreo cookies, and ice cream. We ate just about everything my mom had bought in preparation for our visit. We would leave the kitchen table after a meal, go up to my bedroom, lie on the bed, unbutton our waistbands, and humorously moan as we realized how much we had just eaten. However, we were always ready for the next feeding frenzy. The food was so good and so much better than the food served at school. And the time spent at the kitchen table or in the family room talking— and eating—was so relaxing.

At Wellesley, I witnessed numerous students with eating disorders. In our dorm dining room, one of the women who sat at my table was so thin that her bones protruded from her body. She would fiddle with the food on her plate, but would not eat.

When questioned about it, she always said that she had eaten earlier with a friend. Little did I know she was anorexic, until I saw her, skeleton-like in her thinness, rummaging through a garbage can to retrieve an apple core to suck on. There also were two other women who were regulars at my table who would eat and eat and eat. It amazed me how much they could eat and maintain their model-like figures. They claimed to have high metabolisms. I figured out they were bulimic when I heard from the bathroom the disgusting sounds of their vomiting after dinner.

My Greek heritage taught me to never, ever run out of food when you are having people over. Not serving enough food was considered almost sinful. My family adopted this 11th Commandment: "Thou shalt always have leftovers after your guests have overeaten." Hosting a party in my family always involved spending 40 percent of the time preparing the food and table, 10 percent of the time actually eating, and 50 percent of the time cleaning up and wrapping up the leftovers. I am proud of my Greek heritage, but in the food and weight department, it did not serve me well.

Food was a cornerstone for my family. I remember when I moved down to Washington, D.C., after college, my mother flew down to visit me. Tony and I were dating at the time and went to the airport to pick her up. We retrieved her bags, and Tony offered to carry them. I could see he was struggling, and he whispered to me, "What the heck is in this suitcase? It weighs a ton."

When we got home, my mother opened the suitcase and there were about 20 cans of corn! She knew that corn was the only vegetable that Tony liked, and wanted to make sure he had enough.

I laughed and said, "So that is why the suitcase was so heavy."

She smiled and replied, "Do not give me any trouble about it now. Your dad was furious about carrying it. Every buzzer in the airport went off when I was checking in!"

When I was a child, my grandmother and great-aunts would pinch my cheeks when they saw me and say, "Honey, you are too thin. You need to put some meat on those bones." Even though I was a bit overweight according to the charts, they thought I was underweight. After all, in Greek culture, as seen in its art, women with "meat on their bones" were symbols of good health and prosperity.

When I was 14 years old, I visited Thea Katerini, one of my favorite great-aunts. She pinched my cheeks and said, "You finally have some meat on those bones. You look so good, honey." That was when I knew I had a legitimate weight problem!

There is no doubt that obesity is a major problem in this country. So much research shows that as a person's weight increases, his or her risks for numerous health conditions also increase. These risks include coronary heart disease, type 2 diabetes, cancers (endometrial, breast, and colon), high blood pressure, high cholesterol, stroke, liver and gall bladder disease, sleep apnea, respiratory problems, osteoarthritis, and gynecological problems (such as abnormal periods and infertility). The list goes on and on.

Since my parents both died of colon cancer and my sister died of breast cancer, I want to do anything I can to lower my own health risks. I am certain that, coupled with their lack of exercise, the excessive weight of both my mother and father contributed to their early deaths.

Dieting had become an obsession for my family. My parents would try to lose weight, but gained back any they had lost. Likewise, my sister's weight was like a yo-yo. She would smoke and fast, but as soon as she tried to quit smoking or stop fasting, she would gain all the weight back. At age 14, I began to try just about anything to lose weight, too. I ate only grapefruit. I took cider vinegar tablets. I tried over-the-counter diet pills. I would lose some weight only to gain it back, just like the other members of my family.

In my mid-thirties, after my mother's death, I was prescribed an antidepressant medication and (unhelpfully) ate to deal with stress. The side effects of the medication, coupled with the stress eating, caused me to gain 40 pounds over seven years. After failing again on more crazy diets, I finally decided to join Weight Watchers, and over the next three years, proceeded to lose those 40 pounds. More than 15 years have passed, and I have kept the weight off.

A major breakthrough for me was replacing the word "diet" in my vocabulary with the concept of making healthy food choices. Dieting needs to become a new lifelong way of thinking, not just a temporary effort. Otherwise, as soon as you go back to your old ways, you

You do not need to "die-it;" you need to "live-it."

gain weight back. You do not need to "die-it;" you need to "live-it." This concept may seem corny, but psychologically it has made a difference for me.

Here are some additional tips I have learned over the years through my weight management journey.

THE KEYS TO MY WEIGHT WATCHER PROGRAM

- Eat at least five servings of fruits and vegetables a day. Some examples of a serving: one cup of leafy greens or half a cup of most other vegetables or fruit.

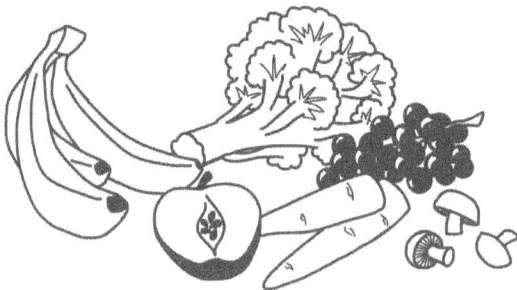

- Add whole grains to your diet every day.

- Eat at least two servings of lean protein a day. Some examples of a serving: two to three ounces of meat, fish, poultry, or tofu; an egg; or one-half cup of lentils or beans.

- Have at least two servings of nonfat or low-fat (one percent) milk or dairy products a day, three if you are over 50 years old. Nonfat yogurt and nonfat milk are lower in calories and still great sources of protein. Some examples of a serving: one cup of milk, one cup of yogurt, or one ounce of hard cheese.

- Drink at least six glasses of nonalcoholic, noncaloric liquids a day.

- Include at least two teaspoons of healthy oils, such as olive or canola oil, in your meals each day.

- Take a multivitamin supplement every day.

- Limit your intake of sugar, sodium, and alcohol. Women should limit their intake of alcohol to no more than one alcoholic beverage per day.

- Eat filling foods to trick your body into thinking your appetite has been satisfied. Items that contain a lot of water, such as fruits, vegetables, and broth-based soups, work well, as do fibrous and lean protein foods, such as oatmeal, chicken, and nonfat Greek plain yogurt. Eight ounces of Greek yogurt have 20 grams of protein. If you cannot stand the taste of plain yogurt, add fruit or some honey to sweeten it. That is better than buying fruit-flavored yogurt that contains added sugar.

- Manage your portions. To estimate an individual portion size visually, think: one ounce of cheese is the size of your thumb, three ounces of meat is the size of a deck of cards, one cup of rice is the size of your fist. These portions may seem extremely small, but that is how serving sizes are defined by national standards.

- If you lose half a pound, do not dismiss it–celebrate it! You are going in the right direction and can think of it as losing the equivalent of two sticks of butter from your body. Obviously, you do not want to use this analogy if you gain half a pound, as that might depress you. In that case, think of the half-pound as a cup of water, which will seem like nothing. Tricky reasoning, I admit, but psychologically helpful.

- Add some activity (exercise) to your life!

HELPFUL FOOD GUIDELINES

- Try to eat at least one of these three "power proteins" each day: eggs, soy, and cheese. Studies have shown that eating two eggs a day helps women lose 65 percent more weight and 83 percent more belly fat than eating a bagel of equal calories. Snacking on protein-rich soy foods, such as soy chips, can initiate weight loss in as few as three days. In addition, studies have found that daily servings of nonfat or low-fat dairy products are markedly effective in accelerating fat loss.

- Eat fiber. Choose foods with at least two grams of fiber per serving. Fiber is a great aid to weight loss, as it makes you feel fuller with fewer calories.

- Avoid trans fats, such as fried foods and packaged baked goods, which increase your bad (low-density lipoprotein, or LDL) cholesterol and decrease your good (high-density lipoprotein, or HDL) cholesterol. Avoid foods that contain partially hydrogenated oils, which is just another name for trans fats.

- Look for snack health bars that have no more than 15 grams of sugar and at least 3 grams of fiber.

- Include some healthy fat in your daily diet. Avoid foods high in saturated fats, such as butter. Instead, choose foods containing unsaturated fats, both monounsaturated and polyunsaturated. Olive oil is about 75 percent monounsaturated fat. Canola oil and cashews are both about 60 percent monounsaturated fat. Other sources include avocados, peanut butter, olives, and nuts. Good sources for polyunsaturated fats include soybean oil, salmon, sunflower seeds, and walnuts.

- Bring a container of cherry or grape tomatoes to work. They are a great source of vitamin C and taste great at room temperature.

- Freeze grapes and also peeled bananas. They are wonderful frozen treats that taste great, are healthy, and take longer to eat, so you feel fuller sooner.

HELPFUL FOOD SUBSTITUTIONS

- Choose all-fruit preserves instead of butter, margarine, or sugared jelly for your spread.

- Top a baked potato with nonfat yogurt, instead of sour cream.

- Dip your bread in olive oil, instead of spreading on butter.

BOOST YOUR METABOLISM

- Include black pepper in your diet. It can act as a diuretic to eliminate excess water weight and boost your metabolic rate.

- Eat foods that contain the natural food compound glutathione, which supports energy production and enhances the immune system. Glutathione can be found in grapefruit, oranges, winter squash, tomatoes, and potatoes.

- Eat watermelon, as it contains the amino acid, arginine, that boosts metabolism.

- Sprinkle one to three teaspoons of cayenne pepper a day into your food. Capsaicin, the active ingredient in spicy peppers, can increase your metabolic rate by 25 percent.

- Sprinkle one-quarter teaspoon of cinnamon into your coffee, tea, cereal, or soup each day. Cinnamon's active compound methylhydroxy chalcone polymer increases glucose metabolism twentyfold and prevents blood sugar dips that trigger carbohydrate cravings.

- Include lemons in your diet. Lemon-rich dishes and drinks can reduce water weight and belly fat. Lemon induces the production of bile, a fluid secreted by the liver that speeds the metabolism of fats and toxins. Squeezing a lemon wedge into a mug of hot water to drink produces the best results. When at a restaurant, ask for lemon in your water.

- Chew sugar-free gum. Researchers have discovered that chewing sugar-free gum all day increases your metabolic rate by about 20 percent. That could burn off more than 10 pounds a year.

DRINK RESPONSIBLY

- Drink a glass of water before eating.

- Drink cold water. Ingesting cold water burns more calories than warmer water, so drink a lot of it chilled. However, since cold water can slow down digestion, drink room temperature water when you are eating a meal.

- If you like milk, try drinking a 16-ounce glass for your breakfast. Many people (including me) find that it keeps them satisfied until lunch and gets most of their daily calcium needs taken care of early in the day.

- Try to avoid drinking sodas, even diet sodas, due to their high sugar (or sugar substitute) and high sodium content.

- Do not "drink" calories by ordering alcoholic beverages. Alcohol and dieting do not mix well. Your body processes alcohol first, leaving carbohydrates and fats to get stored as fat instead of getting used as fuel. If you are going to drink alcohol, wine is the lowest-calorie selection, with typically 120 calories per 5-ounce serving. Beer is the next best choice, with about 150 calories per 12-ounce serving. Liqueurs and mixed drinks are generally not low-calorie choices. A typical pina colada contains about 250 calories, which could equal the calories of a lean entrée.

Establish Good Mealtime Habits

- Eat slowly. Put your fork down between bites.

- Keep a food journal to make you aware of what you are eating. I weigh myself weekly and keep a weekly journal between weigh-ins. If I have a good week, I can look back to see what I ate. When I used to get lazy and did not want to keep track, I would say to myself, "Only journal on the days you want to lose weight," and that tended to provide me the needed motivation.

- Visually divide your plate. Try to fill half of the plate with vegetables (or fruit), a quarter of the plate with protein, and a quarter of the plate with whole grains.

- When going out to dinner, decide ahead of time that when you have finished half your meal, you will ask for a take-out box and pack the other half to bring home and enjoy for lunch the next day. Also, ask for your salad dressings and gravies on the side.

- Stop eating and walk to the restroom halfway through your meal, even if you do not need to go. This interruption will give your brain the time it needs to catch up to how your stomach is feeling.

- Eat breakfast. Studies show better weight loss when you eat breakfast. The sooner you eat in the day, the sooner your body begins to burn calories and fat.

- Do not starve yourself. Eating too little slows down your metabolism, as your body goes into "starvation mode" and tries to conserve energy.

Food & Mood Journal

Date: _____   Mon   Tue   Wed   Thurs   Fri   Sat   Sun   Weight: _____

Check # 8 ounce glasses of water: ▯ ▯ ▯ ▯ ▯ ▯ ▯ ▯

Time	Place	Food/Beverage	How Much	Mood Before	Mood After

What's your Mood: exhausted, angry, sad, frustrated, stressed, depressed, overwhelmed, anxious, lonely, jealous, bored, hopeful, con dent, happy, thrilled, etc.

My Day in Review: (Times/situations/moods likely to cause cravings, types of food most likely to crave, etc.):
....
....
....

Behaviors that Require my attention: ....
....
....

Notes: ....
....
....

How I did today: ☐ Fabulous   ☐ Great   ☐ OK   ☐ Will Do Better Tomorrow

- Avoid grocery shopping when you are hungry. Eat before you go to the supermarket, or better yet, enjoy a cup of tea or a diet drink before you go to the store.

- Try to stick to the outer aisles in supermarkets. That is where the fresh fruits, vegetables, dairy products, and other healthy items are located. Avoid the middle aisles where cookies, candy, and snacks are stocked.

- On Halloween, purchase candy that you personally do not enjoy. That will decrease the temptation to eat it.

- Make sleep a priority. Studies have shown that women who do not get enough sleep are one-third more likely than those who do get enough sleep to experience a weight gain of about two pounds per year. Sleep will provide you the energy to exercise and the willpower to stick to a healthy diet. Most doctors suggest at least seven to eight hours of sleep a night. If that is not possible, try to fit in some quick naps during the day.

CRASH YOUR CRAVINGS

- Suck a menthol or eucalyptus cough drop to stop cravings.

- If at night you are prone to cravings, go brush and floss your teeth early in the evening. The fact that your teeth are clean can discourage you from eating.

- Go outside for a walk.

- Go into another room or do a chore. Most cravings will subside within five minutes.

Chapter Two
Getting and Staying Fit

M ost members of my family were overweight and did not exercise. My father died at the age of 63, my mother died at the age of 64, and my sister died at the age of 59. I am certain that their poor physical condition played a critical part in ending their lives much too soon.

The facts are well documented. In a recent study published by the American Cancer Society, women who spent six hours a day sitting down increased their risk of early death by 37 percent, compared to those who spent less than three hours a day sitting down. Whether you are in the car, on the sofa, at the office, or in a theater, sitting is not healthy.

Numerous studies also show that less physical activity leaves you more prone to depression, because you have lower levels of endorphins, the feel-good hormones. Exercise may, in fact, be one of the most powerful

strategies for dealing with depression, out-performing antidepressants. I personally have experienced this correlation. I usually feel much better and more energetic after I exercise.

Having witnessed how lack of physical fitness negatively affected and ultimately shortened the lives of my own family members–and having read the scientific studies–I came to realize how important exercise is to me and to anyone who wants to live a long, healthy life.

At Wellesley College during the mid-1970s, I did not see many women exercising. During those years, there were not many role models for women in sports. Jane Fonda, the first woman I remember to publicly promote health and fitness in videos, was not yet on the scene, and Jack LaLanne, the fitness and nutrition expert who was on the scene, just did not "cut it" as a role model for young women. Women at Wellesley often saw exercise as something you should not take time away from studying to do. At that stage of my life, studying and socializing with friends were far more important to me.

Unfortunately, I did not go to Wellesley with a habit of exercise in place. I know that the Greeks invented the Olympics, and you would think that the requirement to stay healthy and fit would be passed down through the generations, but not in my family. I cannot remember many times when my mother or father got off the couch without saying, "Ooh, my body hurts." Sitting seemed to be the position that I saw most in our extended family: aunts around the kitchen table talking, uncles sitting in the living room catching up on the sports teams, and children sitting around a table coloring and obeying their parents' instructions to be quiet and behaved. When I visited Greece in 2009, the same tendency seemed to hold true: women sitting outside talking, men sitting in the bars watching a soccer game, and children sitting and playing a board game.

To avoid this sedentary lifestyle, I have belonged to three workout clubs for many years. They are: Curves, a women-only,

30-minute in-and-out, full-body aerobic and resistance gym; Planet Fitness; and The Workout Club. The two latter ones are co-ed, full-scale gyms. I have also purchased so many infomercial devices and videos that I could open up my own rental library. Do I use these workout clubs, devices, and videos? Definitely not enough. In fact, my son once asked me, "Can I move all the stuff off the treadmill, so I can use it?"

Remember how exercise used to be playtime when we were young? I remember each summer going out to play with friends all day long. We would play baseball, kickball, and hopscotch and go bicycling and swimming. When we were obliged to go home to eat lunch and dinner, we quickly ate the minimum acceptable by our mothers, so that we could get back outside as soon as possible. Each summer, I also spent a week at my grandparents' house in Lynn, Massachusetts. My grandmother would stand me up in a large vat of grapes where I jumped up and down, squishing the grapes to make the family's wine. That experience reminds me of an *I Love Lucy* episode. Little did I know that I was actually helping my grandmother with a chore. Despite the purple toes, it was so much fun!

Oh my goodness, have things changed. At Curves, a poster on the wall says, "We don't stop playing because we get old. We get old because we stop playing." So I have always tried to make exercise fun and include more playtime in my life: playing baseball and touch football out in the yard with the kids, bicycling as a family, participating in work sports teams, and playing tennis with friends. I also try to think of this as "being active" or "enjoying activities in life," instead of "getting exercise."

Do not get caught up in and overwhelmed by the need to go to a gym and exercise at least an hour a day, every day syndrome. The American Heart Association has recommended at least 150 minutes per week of moderate exercise, or 75 minutes per week of vigorous exercise. That is about 11 to 22 minutes per day. Recent research by the National Cancer Institute shows that exercising for just 10 minutes per day can add 1.8 years to your life. Every little bit helps.

I have found that the three keys to keep exercising are taming your fear (not thinking that it is exercise and overwhelming), creating variety (not getting bored), and maintaining structure (forcing yourself to do it). Here are some suggestions for exercising that I have found helpful over the years.

<u>TAME YOUR FEAR</u>

- Buy yourself a pedometer. Just having it on you provides motivation. The average woman takes about 5,200 steps per day. Figure out how many steps you take a day and then gradually add more until you can reach the recommended 10,000 steps per day.

- Leave an extra pair of walking shoes in your car or office and exercise in several short periods throughout the day. For example, park farther from the store entrance, walk to someone's office instead of calling or sending an email, and take a 10-minute walk during lunchtime. Each 10-minute session will increase your energy (and burn calories) for up to two hours and can affect how your body metabolizes blood sugar for up to 72 hours. Multiple short exercise times can be even more effective than one longer time.

- Take the stairs instead of the elevator and take a few of them two-at-a-time for good lunges.

- Stretch at your desk while at work. Interlace your fingers and reach over your head to stretch your wrists, arms and shoulders, and then lean to either side to loosen your back.

- Get up from your desk and walk around at least once every hour.

- From a sitting position, while holding the armrests of your stationary and sturdy desk chair, slowly lower your body in front of it and then return to your original position. These triceps dips will firm your upper arms.

- Make use of your commute time and convert some of it to workout time. For example, the next time you are at a red light, sit up tall with your shoulders back. Inhale as you pull your abs up and in toward your spine. As you hold your stomach in, keep your spine lifted and shoulders back and slowly count to three. Then slowly exhale. Repeat five times or until the light changes. Also, squeeze your butt or tighten your abdominals while you sit at an intersection.

CREATE VARIETY

- Write down all of your exercising options in a notebook, such as: Pilates video, visit to Curves, Zumba class, or 30-minute walk. Each night, pick at least one of them to do the next day. Some hobbies, such as sailing and gardening, offer a great workout. Lifting children and hauling groceries also count as exercise.

- Stretch. Stretching exercises not only can both energize and relax you; they also can help you sleep. In a study done at the Fred Hutchinson Cancer Research Center in Seattle, women who were having trouble sleeping needed 60 percent less sleep medication and had 30 percent less difficulty falling asleep when they stretched four times a week. Try this stretch that can be done anytime, even during television commercials: Stand with your back against a wall, with your feet about a foot away from it, hip-distance apart. Inhale, pull your

35

stomach in, and press your entire back against the wall. As you exhale, roll your head, neck, shoulders, and upper back slowly forward and downward, until only your tailbone and rear are still touching the wall. Relax your neck and shoulders and let your head and arms hang. Take deep, slow breaths. Circle your arms inward five times, then outward five times. Slowly roll back up.

- Flatten your belly with a simple stretch and yoga pose called Downward-Facing Dog. Crouch on all fours. Keeping your palms and toes on the floor, both hip-width apart, slowly straighten your arms and legs until you have pressed and lifted up your bottom into the air. Hold for four breaths, then release.

- For great push-ups, lean into the wall with your hands shoulder-width apart and push back out. Repeat 10 times. If you do this daily, you will notice increasing strength in your upper arms.

- To trim thighs, try balletic pliés. Stand with your feet shoulder-width apart and pointing outward. Bend your knees and lower your body straight down until your thighs are parallel to the floor. Then stand back up. Try to repeat at least 10 times.

- Looking for replacements for exercise gadgets? Try these:
  o Instead of buying a machine to strengthen your thighs, take a slightly deflated ball–such as a volleyball, basketball, or soccer ball–place it between your knees and squeeze.
  o Instead of buying a bow exercise machine to strengthen your arms and chest, stretch a resistance band in front of you.

o   Instead of buying a machine to "roll your buns and thighs," lie flat on the floor with your knees bent and heels on top of a stability ball. Raise your hips and roll the ball toward you, then slowly return to the starting position. Repeat 10 times.

MAINTAIN STRUCTURE

- Write "Exercise" in your calendar. For example, make an entry for "Exercise" every Monday, Wednesday, and Friday from 6 to 7 p.m. But be flexible.

- Do not exercise when you are feeling bad. According to the American College of Sports Medicine, if you have a minor cold, light workouts will not worsen your symptoms. However, if you have a fever, more intense workouts can hinder your immune system. Wait until you are feeling better, before you resume any running or weightlifting program.

- Stop thinking of excuses not to exercise, such as, "I just do not have the time." I doubt you have ever said after a workout, "That was a waste of time."

- Sign up for regularly scheduled events. For example, reserve an hour at an indoor tennis court during the winter months or arrange with a friend to walk on certain days and times.

- Decide to spend at least one commercial break during a television show doing some sort of exercise, such as sit-ups, lunges, or jogging in place.

Chapter Three
Energy Boosts

L ife at Wellesley College required an abundance of energy. The courses were demanding and involved many hours of classroom time and many late nights of studying. Participation in campus events and clubs was also expected. And on weekends, you would need to travel to Harvard or MIT to try to meet men.

Many Wellesley women chose to drink coffee for energy. Others used a stock of amphetamines. I did not like the taste of coffee and I feared the effects of drugs. I would say to myself, "Okay, what would give me a lift and energize me?" In the spring, that would be a Red Sox game! I would take the bus from Wellesley to MIT, ride the T (Boston's mass transit system) to Fenway Park, pay $1 for a bleacher ticket (yes, $1 for a ticket), run up the stairs to my seat, and

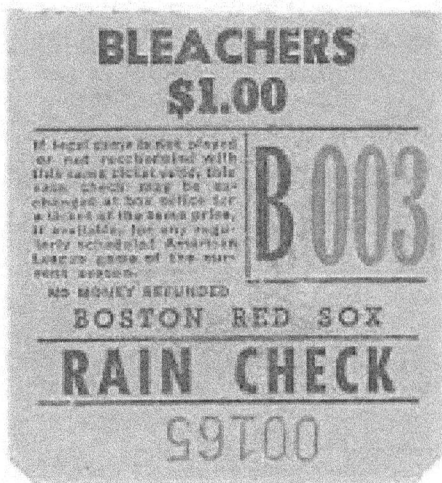

BLEACHERS $1.00

If this game is not played or not rescheduled with this same ticket used, this rain check may be exchanged at box office for a ticket of the same price, if available, for any regularly scheduled American League game of the current season.

NO MONEY REFUNDED

B003

BOSTON RED SOX

RAIN CHECK

59T00

cheer on my beloved baseball team. Those outings provided me with the break I needed from the Wellesley routine and energized me for days. Your equivalent cure might be going to a concert or calling a friend. It is funny how doing something you love can provide you with the boost you need.

It is funny how doing something you love can provide you with the boost you need.

Given all of the expectations and responsibilities in our lives, it is no wonder why "I am tired" tends to be a common phrase in our lexicon and a common response to someone asking you how you are. A few years ago, when I was exercising at Curves, one of the other women on the circuit said, "I am so tired of being tired." How depressing is that! Anything that can provide you an energy lift should be greatly appreciated and prized. Here are some ideas that I have found helpful.

<u>FOODS FOR ENERGY</u>

- Eat orange or red fruits and vegetables. Eating mangoes, apricots, carrots, and tomatoes can reduce tiredness by more than 50 percent.

- When traveling, take 150 mg of pine bark extract before and after a flight. It can alleviate jet lag by 50 percent.

- Eat foods rich in the amino acid tyrosine. Tyrosine is found in soy products, chicken, turkey, fish, peanuts, almonds, avocados, bananas, milk, cheese, yogurt, cottage cheese, lima beans, pumpkin seeds, and sesame seeds. Tyrosine allows your brain to synthesize the neurotransmitters dopamine and norepinephrine, which help keep your mind attentive and alert.

- Eat protein. The midafternoon slump is well documented. Why else do numerous countries have an afternoon siesta as part of their cultures? However, here in the United States, the common response seems to be reaching for a caffeinated drink or a sugary snack. If you cannot take a power nap, research suggests that a good serving of protein at lunch, such as tuna or chicken, will help you overcome your afternoon tiredness without the rollercoaster energy trip of coffee.

- Eat foods rich in magnesium, or take a magnesium supplement. Magnesium plays a critical role in your body's performance in converting glucose to energy. A low magnesium level can produce a lack of energy.

- Eat bananas. In addition to providing valuable nutrients, including potassium, vitamin C, and vitamin B6, bananas are a good source of carbohydrates and are simple, high energy, and easy to digest.

- Eat yogurt or drink milk. Milk and milk products are excellent sources of carbohydrates and protein, plus they provide the calcium to help build strong bones. Stick to low-fat or nonfat dairy products for easier digestion and to limit saturated fat.

- Eat peanut butter, peanuts, and other nuts. They provide fuel and sustained energy from a combination of protein and carbohydrates. Their healthy heart-protecting fats keep you going over the long haul.

- Eat oatmeal. It is digested slowly and offers sustained energy. For more substance, add dried or fresh fruit, milk, and nuts. Try whole oats, rather than instant or rolled oats, to max out the time it takes to digest them.

- Eat beans. They are a great source of both protein and carbohydrates. Toss them into salads, soups, and pasta dishes. One of my favorite snacks is hummus and pita bread, because it combines legumes, healthy fats, and carbohydrates into one very portable package.

- Eat dried fruit. Some people shy away from it, because of its calories. However, its portability and nutrient density make it a healthy choice. Keep it in your desk and in your car for energy emergencies.

ACTIVITIES TO INCREASE ENERGY

- Soak up some sun. Exposure to bright light in the morning can boost energy throughout the day and improve your mood. Light stimulates neurotransmitters in your brain, such as dopamine and serotonin, which boost your spirits and increase motivation. Even a cloudy day offers enough natural light to have a stimulating effect on your brain. Also, a lamp that reproduces the clear full-spectrum light of the sun can help. For a sure lift, use it in the morning while you do your exercises.

- Go outside and take some deep breaths. Even if it is cloudy, or even if you just sit, breathing in fresh air is good for you.

- Stop working, sit down, drink a glass of water or a cup of tea, and do nothing for five minutes.

- Phone someone who makes you laugh.

- Move. A brisk walk around the block or even two minutes of stretching at your desk improves blood flow and boosts energy.

- Drink at least eight glasses of water per day. A dehydrated body functions less efficiently. Keep bottled water at your desk and offer it to visitors, instead of coffee.

- Limit your caffeine use. For most healthy adults, moderate doses of caffeine–200 to 300 mg or about two to four cups of brewed coffee a day–are not likely to cause harm. However, heavy daily caffeine use–more than 500 to 600 milligrams a day–may cause insomnia, nervousness, restlessness, and irritability.

- Do not skip meals. Going without food for too long allows blood sugar levels to dip. Try to eat something at least every five hours to maintain your energy levels throughout the day. Always pack a snack to take with you when you are on the go.

Chapter Four
Looking Good

I remember in the movie, *My Big Fat Greek Wedding*, Toula's father, Gus Portokalos, thought that Windex was the cure for all problems, including pimples. In my Greek family, we believed the cure-all was olive oil. Olive oil on your face and neck to prevent wrinkles, olive oil on the scalp to prevent dandruff, olive oil on the body to prevent dryness, olive oil to cure just about any health problem you might have.

When I was a young girl, each and every time one great-aunt visited, she brought multiple bottles of extra virgin olive oil. She lived in Boston and had access to numerous Greek supermarkets that definitely were not present in Somersworth, New Hampshire. When she arrived, she would open one of the bottles and begin to rub the oil on my arms, neck, and face, saying, "Honey, this will keep you soft and young." I had no choice but to accept her spa treatment. She provided additional layers of the magic oil numerous times during her stay. I would go upstairs to the bathroom, rubbing it in to remove the shine, but being careful not to make it appear that it was wiped off. I did not want to offend my aunt, and I certainly did not want to look like I was due for another treatment!

45

One evening during one of her visits, I planned to go to the movies with a friend. When she came in our front door and saw me, she said, "Wow, your skin looks nice. It has an olive glow to it. It must be those Greek genes." I glanced at my aunt, and she gave me a proud smile and nod to confirm yet again the importance of olive oil. However, later during the movie, my friend turned to me and asked, "Do you smell salad?"

The following tips are for women who want to take good care of their skin, hair, teeth, and nails and to manage their wardrobes well, so that they can feel confident they look their best.

ENHANCE YOUR EYES

- If you are under the age of 40, use eyelash products that enhance lash length. However, if you are over the age of 40, use eyelash products that pump up the volume. Although we all are born with three rows of upper eyelashes, by the age of 50, lashes naturally dwindle to a single row.

- Put eyeliner pencil in the freezer for 15 minutes to avoid crumbling it when you sharpen it.

BEAUTIFY YOUR TEETH AND NAILS

- To remove stains from your teeth, crush a strawberry to a pulp and mix it with half a teaspoon of baking powder. Spread the mixture onto your teeth, wait five minutes, spit it out, and then brush thoroughly with toothpaste. The malic acid in strawberries removes surface discoloration.

- Keep your cuticles moisturized by dabbing on some oil, such as olive oil, with a cotton swab.

- Floss your teeth as well as brushing them. No matter how well you think you brush, you miss about 40 percent of tooth surfaces. Brushing and flossing are especially critical at night, to avoid plaque, tartar, and germs from remaining on your teeth and gums while you sleep. Otherwise, these deposits could lead to gingivitis, which is a major cause of inflammation.

- To remove those stains that remain when you remove dark nail polish, take two tooth-whitening strips and cut each one into five nail-size pieces. Apply them to your nails for 20 minutes and repeat daily, if needed, until the stains are gone. The hydrogen peroxide in the strips gently restores your nails' natural color.

HANDLE YOUR HAIR

- Prevent hair loss by massaging your scalp for five minutes every day to stimulate circulation.

- Avoid washing your hair every day. Just rinse with water every other day.

- Run a fabric softener sheet over your hair for better control of static electricity.

IMPROVE YOUR SKIN

- Use a cotton cosmetic pad dampened with apple cider vinegar to tone your skin.

- Eat berries, such as cranberries, blueberries, strawberries, and raspberries. The ellagic acid they contain can prevent premature aging of your skin.

- Use a skin moisturizer with sunscreen 365 days per year, to lower your risk of skin cancer.

- Give yourself a weekly tomato facial. Take half of a tomato and massage it over your face. Tomatoes contain lycopene, which is naturally astringent and anti-inflammatory. It can prevent adult acne.

- Use apple cider vinegar to remove skin tags, moles, or warts. Apply it with a cotton ball two to three times a day for a week.

- Drink green tea and eight glasses of water per day, to heal damaged skin cells.

- Use ice and toothpaste to heal pimples. Ice improves blood circulation, freezes the pores, and helps to remove excess oils and dirt from the skin. Wrap an ice cube in a piece of cloth and apply it to the pimple for about five minutes. Then apply a pinch of toothpaste and leave it on for 20 minutes. Wash it off with icy cold water.

- Use retinol, which is found in many skin care products. It can increase cellular rejuvenation, reduce wrinkles, and unclog and smooth skin to keep you looking young and pimple-free.

- Applying lemon juice twice daily will lighten or remove age spots over several weeks. Lemons have highly acidic juice that helps peel off layers of your skin.

- Age spots are one of the most common complaints of women as we age. These spots (also known as liver spots, sunspots, or lentigines) are caused by sun exposure. Protect your skin with a sunscreen that has a sun protection factor (SPF) of at least 15. Wear hats when outside and cover up with clothing when it is practical to do so. Remember, though reduced, the sun's rays also penetrate your skin when it is cloudy.

- Exfoliation is the process of removing surface cells that tend to be dark. This increases skin cell renewal, which promotes softer skin, fades age spots, and helps even out skin tone. After a bath or shower, try using a slightly abrasive towel to gently brush your face and body. Various exfoliation techniques also can be performed by professional aestheticians.

- Your pharmacy can provide makeup formulated specifically for hiding spots or covering scars.

- Add olive oil to your bath to soften dry skin.

- For dry, cracked heels, rinse your feet with warm water at bedtime and massage olive oil or a dab of vegetable shortening onto the problem spots. Then pull on a pair of thick cotton socks and leave on overnight. The fatty acids in the oil lubricate dry, callused heels while locking in your skin's own moisture.

- Keep your hands moisturized with lotion from a bottle by your sink. Apply lotion after you wash, while your skin is still damp, to lock in moisture. For very rough skin, coat your hands with petroleum jelly or olive oil, pull on some gloves, and let your hands moisturize overnight. When drying your hands, blot rather than rub them.

- How to have a great wardrobe on a small budget
  - o Consider renting from sites, such as www.lendingluxury. com, that lend out designer clothes for less than 15 percent of the garments' cost and sell slightly used clothes for 80 percent off retail.
  - o Find yourself a "fashion friend." If you are fortunate to have a friend who wears the same size clothes or shoes that you do, ask if she is interested in sharing wardrobes.

- How your wardrobe can help you look thinner
  - o Find a good fit. Clothes that are too tight or too baggy will make you appear larger. Avoid bulky sweaters and sweatshirts.
  - o Choose darker, solid colors, such as black, navy blue, and gray.
  - o Dress monochromatically¬–all in one color–top to bottom, with no patterns.
  - o If you want to wear patterns, go for smaller ones.
  - o Avoid horizontal stripes. Look for thin vertical or diagonal lines, instead. They will help you look taller and thinner. If you are "vertically challenged" as I am at five feet, one inch tall, you especially will appreciate stripes.
  - o Avoid pleats near the waist. Flat-front pants and skirts provide a slimming effect.
  - o Avoid shiny fabrics, such as velour and satin.
  - o Forego the frills. Extra ruffles and material only add bulk.
  - o Choose open collar shirts, V-neck shirts, and scoop necklines to make your torso appear taller.
  - o Avoid small handbags. Stick with a medium-size bag in proportion to your body.

- o Limit your use of white, since it can make you look larger. Wearing white slacks or panty hose can add bulk to your appearance.
- o For your most flattering profile, any professional photographer would ask you to position your hips at a 45-degree angle to the camera, rotate your shoulders toward it, shift your weight to your back foot, lean your body slightly forward, crane your neck, drop your chin half an inch, and put your hand on your front hip with your elbow as far back as it will go. Phew! I am not sure if all that is really worth it.

- How to make your legs look longer and thinner
  - o Wear skirts that fall right above the knee.
  - o Wear dark panty hose and stay away from patterned leggings.
  - o Match your belt and shoes to your skirt or pants.
  - o Opt for an asymmetrical, tiered skirt.

- Choose colors with care
  - o Darker colors (reds or burgundies, browns, blues, greens, or grays) are for occasions when you want to be taken seriously.
  - o Black (which symbolizes authority) and red or burgundy (which symbolizes power) are the strongest colors. Dark clothes can look conservative yet sexy, making you appear thinner and giving your self-esteem a turbo-boost.
  - o Navy blue (which symbolizes leadership) is also a power color and good to wear to important meetings.
  - o Green (which symbolizes neutrality) can be effective when you have to play the role of a mediator or facilitator. Wearing green can convey down-to-earth, natural beauty, and that while somewhat stubborn, you are someone who likes to have fun.

- o Pastel colors (light blues, pinks, oranges, or yellows) are for every day, when you want to appear approachable.
- o Blue expresses that you are fun-loving, independent, and comfortable with yourself and your achievements.
- o Pink conveys that you are traditional, charming, and feminine. A pink and black combo is a trendy twosome for women who like to add mystery to their otherwise girly image.
- o Orange suggests that you are extroverted and gutsy, that you like to stand out in a crowd and enjoy new challenges.
- o Yellow communicates that you are optimistic, athletic, and outdoorsy, that you have a vibrant personality and great intuition.
- o White implies that you like to be safe and are risk-averse; you favor colors that will not clash with any other part of your outfit. White can be a great accent for tanned or dark skin, adding sex appeal to the "colorless" color.

- Wear hoop earrings that complement your face shape
  - o Square face: Try large hoops that extend just below your chin, to soften the angle of your strong jaw.
  - o Round face: Try a dainty column of stacked loops, to create a vertical line that elongates your face.
  - o Full face: Try connected loops hovering one inch above your shoulders, to pull viewers' eyes downward and away from your cherubic cheeks.

- Handle Wardrobe Emergencies
  - o Do not have the time to hem those pants? Make cuffs or fold material under and secure with double-sided tape, called "bachelor's stitches."
  - o Pants too tight to button? Wear a top that will cover the waistband. Then thread one end of an elastic band

through the pants' buttonhole, thread it back through the loop of its other end, and attach it to the button.

o   Zipper stuck? Use a cotton swab to apply a drop of olive oil to lubricate the teeth. The zipper should move up and down freely.

o   Shoes wet?   Stuff crumpled paper in them to dry overnight.

o   Dress keeps falling on the closet floor? Attach a couple of pieces of Velcro to the ends of the hanger to keep thin straps from sliding off.

o   Needle and thread get tangled when sewing? Before you begin, poke a threaded needle through a fabric softener sheet and run it through.

o   Necklace too long for that outfit?   Pinch the chain to your desired length and fasten a small safety pin through the links at that point.

o   Necklace tangled? Massage a drop of olive oil onto the tangled area and then carefully use a straight pin to pull the knot apart.

o   Food items making a mess of your purse? Store your mints, gum, and cough drops in a clear Ziploc bag. They will be easier to find and will not melt onto other items in your purse.

Chapter Five
Health and Wellness

L iving a long and healthy life is probably the biggest obsession I have. I want to live long enough to see my sons, Matthew and David, get married, and I want to have time with my future grandchildren. Since my dad, mom, and sister died of cancer at the ages of 63, 64, and 59 respectively, I am a bit obsessed about trying to stay healthy. Maybe "terrified" is the better word for describing how I feel. My dad died when Matthew was 19 months old, and Matthew has no memories of him. Matthew was six years old and David was two years old when my mom died; Matthew has very limited memories of her and David has none. It saddens me when I think of all the years that have passed when my sons could have been enjoying and making memories with my mom and dad. It also saddens me that my mom and dad were deprived of time with their grandchildren. I do not want that to happen to me.

Throughout my life, I have confronted many serious health problems in my family: My mom with her high blood pressure, diabetes, obesity, and then cancer; my dad with his kidney stones, smoking, obesity, and then cancer; and my sister with her smoking, eating disorders, drug abuse, and then cancer.

I guess what frightens me the most is how, in a split second, your life can change forever. On the day my mom was having experimental surgery at Massachusetts General Hospital, my

In a split second, your life can change forever. office administrative assistant came to me and said, "The doctor is on the phone; the surgery is over." I vividly remember staring at that phone, knowing that as soon as I picked it up, I would find out whether there was hope or not. I hesitated. When I slowly picked up the phone, I heard my mom's doctor say, "Bad news, Val. The surgery was not successful, and unfortunately there are no other options. I'm sorry." My life then changed forever. For years I have rewound that moment, hoping that when I picked up the phone, I would hear, "Good news, Val! The surgery went well and it's looking good."

I also have faced crises with my own health, waiting to hear if the breast growth was cancerous, if the stomach ultrasound identified a colon problem, if the persistent cough was lung disease. Luckily so far, tense moments like these have ended with good news.

Soon before my husband, Tony, retired as a mathematical statistician from the UMass Center for Survey Research, he worked with a group of research gerontologists–doctors who study the process of aging. These doctors believe that practicing the traditional Chinese martial art of Tai Chi starting at the age of 60 will prolong a person's life by an average of five years. They needed a study to be done to prove their theory and publish their findings. Within a month of hearing this, I began Tai Chi lessons, and now Tony has joined me.

Because of my dedication to living a long life, I have always read just about everything I can about achieving and maintaining good health. Here are the findings that have been most helpful to me.

COMBAT CANCER

- Strawberries contain ellagic acid, known to be a potent cancer-fighter.

- Limonoids in grapefruit help your immune system detoxify the compounds that cause breast cancer. Grapefruits are rich in limonoids and also in naringin, which in laboratory studies stopped the growth of breast cancer cells. Grapefruit can also protect against prostate cancer. Red grapefruits tend to be more wholesome than white grapefruits, since they contain more of a compound called lycopene, known to fight heart disease, cancer, and asthma. Be careful, though, as some prescription drugs state not to eat grapefruit while taking them. Consult your doctor.

- Eating just 28 grams of fiber each day can lower your risk of getting breast cancer by almost 40 percent.

- Cruciferous vegetables, such as broccoli, cauliflower, and cabbage, contain phytonutrients known as glucosinolates, which may help inhibit the metabolism of some carcinogens and stimulate your body's production of detoxification enzymes.

- Eating too much sugar can increase your risk of pancreatic cancer. Drinking more than two sugary sodas a day can nearly double your odds of getting pancreatic cancer.

- Soy-found in soy nuts, tofu, and miso soup-contains phytoestrogens, which act like estrogen blockers and produce similar effects as tamoxifen, the anticancer drug.

- Green tea is rich in epigallocatechin gallate (EGCG), a powerful antioxidant that not only inhibits the growth of cancer cells, but also kills cancer cells without harming healthy tissue. Drinking two to three cups of green tea a day can reduce your risk of esophageal cancer by half.

- Turmeric may prevent and slow the growth of a number of types of cancer, particularly tumors of the esophagus, mouth, intestines, stomach, breast, and skin.

- Patients receiving chemotherapy to treat breast cancer complete more of their therapy when aerobic exercise or resistance training is part of their regime. These physical workouts improve their fitness and self-esteem.

ATTACK ASTHMA

- If you have an attack that leaves your chest tight, drink coffee when you first start wheezing to give you some relief.

- A New Zealand study found that adults eating the staples of the Mediterranean Diet—fish, nuts, and olive oil—for 12 weeks had better control of their asthma symptoms.

- Eating apples can help, as they contain kellin, a compound that works to keep your airways open.

- Munching on Brazil nuts helps asthma sufferers breathe more easily.

BRING DOWN BLOOD PRESSURE

- Eating blueberries can lower your blood pressure. Anthocyanin, an antioxidant in blueberries, relaxes your arterial walls, improving circulation to help regulate blood pressure.

- Eating celery can lower your blood pressure. Celery contains the chemical butylphthalide, which soothes the muscles lining blood vessels and allows for easier blood flow at lower pressures.

CUT CHOLESTEROL

- Keep your LDL (low-density lipoprotein) or "bad" cholesterol below 130 and your HDL (high-density lipoprotein) or "good" cholesterol above 65. Limit dietary cholesterol to no more than 300 mg a day.

- Great sources of cholesterol-lowering omega-3 fatty acids can be found in salmon, soybeans, walnuts, and flaxseed.

- Eating beets can lower LDL cholesterol by 40 percent in 16 weeks and also increase HDL cholesterol. The beta-cyanin in beets promotes the breakdown of artery-clogging triglycerides in your blood.

- Pears contain an insoluble fiber called lignin, which acts like Velcro, attaching to the cholesterol in your body and carrying it out of your system, so you do not absorb it.

- Almonds can lower your LDL, as well as cut your risk of heart attacks. People who snack on nuts at least four times a week cut their risk of fatal heart attacks. Soy nuts have 25 percent fewer calories than nuts; they also have one-third more protein and twice the fiber of peanuts.

- Chocolate can raise HDL (good cholesterol), lower LDL (bad cholesterol), lower blood pressure, and decrease the risk of blood clots due to its abundance of antioxidants called flavonoids. However, chocolate also has its dark sides—no pun intended. If you are sensitive to caffeine, note that a typical milk chocolate bar contains 10 mg of caffeine, and a dark chocolate bar contains 30 mg of caffeine. To put that into perspective, a typical cup of coffee contains about 100 mg of caffeine. Also, chocolate can cause havoc for calorie-counters. It contains about 150 calories per ounce and is considered a "trigger food," meaning that once you start eating it, it can be hard to stop. So enjoy it in moderation. Buy dark chocolate with 70 percent or more cocoa solids and avoid chocolate with milk fat, partially hydrogenated oil, or palm kernel oil.

COPE WITH COLDS AND FLU

- Taking magnesium (200 mg twice a day) provides relief from coughing.

- The compound theobromine found in dark chocolate is more effective at suppressing coughs than codeine. It calms your agitated vagus nerve that triggers coughs.

- If you have congested sinuses, massage the "Yingxiang" acupressure points located beside each of your nostrils for 30 seconds to clear out your sinus cavity.

- Echinacea (900 mg per day) and zinc (50 mg per day) can help shorten the time of a cold.

- Flus cannot be prevented, but you can shave off a few days of suffering by taking elderberry or its extract, Sambucol.

- Research shows that chicken soup, the "Jewish penicillin," actually works. Studies show that some ingredient in the soup blocks or slows the amount of mucus congregating in the lung area and relieves congestion.

- Take a 500-mg garlic supplement two to three times a day to give you some germ resistance.

- When you have a sore throat or laryngitis, clearing your throat is the worst thing you can do. Instead, suck lozenges and sip water to keep your throat moistened. Replace your toothbrush every six months or at the first sign of a sore throat.

- Wipe clean your phones, computer keyboards, remote controls, and refrigerator door handles every week with an antibacterial cleanser.

- Wash your hands frequently. Your hands are a major means of spreading germs. Have a small bottle of antibacterial gel with you and use it frequently. Sneeze or cough into your arms or sleeves, rather than into your hands.

AID DIGESTION

- Drinking a six-ounce glass of red or white wine can relieve diarrhea and Irritable Bowel Syndrome (IBS). If you have diarrhea, also try the BRAT diet to relieve it: Bananas, Rice, Applesauce, and Toast.

- To avoid having gas, drink herbal tea containing peppermint and caraway oils to settle your stomach and aid digestion.

- To stop heartburn, eat pasta, potatoes, rice, or other foods high in complex carbohydrates, which will absorb the acid in your stomach.

- Ginger can speed digestion, so finish off a meal with a bit of candied ginger or sprinkle powdered ginger into your coffee or tea. It moves food quickly into your small intestine and lessens stomach discomfort after a big meal.

- To relieve nausea and motion sickness, try five minutes of pressure on the "Nei Guan" or Pericardium 6 (P6) acupressure points, located on the inside center of your lower arms, three fingers' width above your wrists.

EAT MORE FIBER

- Eating a morning meal rich in fiber may make you more alert during the day. People who eat cereal packed with 6 to 12 grams of fiber in the morning can experience a 10 percent reduction in fatigue, have fewer memory problems, feel less depressed, and fall asleep faster.

- Soluble fiber slows down the absorption of food in your gastrointestinal tract, thereby providing a feeling of fullness. It also can help reduce blood cholesterol levels. Good sources of soluble fiber include dry beans, lentils, peas, and fresh fruits and vegetables.

- Insoluble fiber, used in certain laxatives, speeds up the movement of food through your gastrointestinal tract. Good sources of insoluble fiber include whole grain breads, bran cereals, and brown rice.

<u>INCLUDE HEALTHY FOODS IN YOUR DIET</u>

- Flaxseed is loaded with compounds that can shield you against heart disease and cancer. Flaxseed lowers cholesterol and shows promise for reversing kidney damage caused by lupus. Consuming one to two tablespoons of ground flaxseed per day can reduce your risk of breast cancer by 64 percent.

- Eating antioxidant-rich foods helps protect you against heart disease and cancer. The top 10 foods with the highest antioxidant content per serving are: blackberries, walnuts, strawberries, artichokes, cranberries, coffee, raspberries, pecans, blueberries, and ground cloves.

- Cucumbers are made up of 90 percent water, and eating them can dissolve kidney and bladder stones, heal stomach ulcers, regulate blood pressure, relieve headaches, and promote healthy skin.

- Eating yogurt can help return your thyroid levels to normal.

- One carrot a day can slash your risk of stroke by almost 70 percent.

- Include enough vitamin D in your diet, take supplements of it, and go outside in the sunshine to produce it naturally.

- Reduce belly fat by avoiding foods with trans fats and limiting sugar to no more than 25 grams a day. As a reference, an average doughnut contains 11 grams of sugar, and an average can of cola contains a whopping 35 grams of sugar. Also, try eating an avocado, an ounce of dark chocolate, or six olives at each meal. Excess belly fat, even in a person of normal weight, nearly doubles your risk of premature death from high blood pressure, heart disease, stroke, and cancer, and can increase your risk of developing dementia. For women, waist circumference should not be more than 34 inches. A tape measure is better than a bathroom scale for assessing your risk.

RELIEVE DISCOMFORT AND PAIN

- If you brushed against poison ivy or poison oak, clean your skin thoroughly with Tecnu, instead of using soap. Tecnu is a chemical product available over-the-counter that breaks up the plant's oil, making it easier to wash off. If blisters appear, treat the itch with calamine lotion and oatmeal baths.

- Mix equal parts of honey, olive oil, and melted beeswax to soothe the burning and itching from rashes, helping them heal more quickly than with cortisone alone.

- Rub an onion on a bee sting or mosquito bite to stop the stinging and itching.

- Take an over-the-counter cough lozenge containing benzocaine to lessen the pain of a burned or bitten tongue.

- Eat foods rich in vitamin C, such as oranges, cantaloupe, broccoli, strawberries, and peppers, to relieve arthritis pain.

- Drink cherry juice to relieve inflammation. When Ludwig W. Blau, Ph.D., reported that eating six cherries every day cured his painful gout, his physician tried the cherry diet on 12 patients and had the same amazing results.

- Run cool, not ice cold, water over a burn to keep it from getting worse. Burns will heal faster if you drink plenty of water and follow a high protein, low sodium diet while you are healing.

- Hold a pinch of instant coffee crystals on a canker sore for immediate pain relief. If you are prone to canker sores, avoid toothpastes that contain sodium lauryl sulfate, often listed as SLS.

- For tiny shaving or paper cuts, use a smudge of lip balm as a sealant. Honey works well on larger cuts and contains ingredients that can speed healing.

- If you have a toothache and are not able to see the dentist right away, try oil of clove for a quick numbing of the area, or chew on a whole clove. Try acupressure by rubbing an ice cube in the V-shaped area between your thumb and index finger on the same side of your body as your aching tooth.

- Use tea tree oil as an antiseptic and disinfectant. As a natural antifungal oil, it helps treat various fungal infections, including acne and athlete's foot.

- Feeling hot from hot flashes or the weather? The back of your neck, wrists, and feet largely control your body heat, so hold a piece of chilled silverware on the back of your neck, hold your wrist against a cold glass of ice water, or swab your feet with an alcohol wipe.

- Try reflexology, an alternative pain treatment in which finger pressure is applied to specific zones and reflex points on your feet, hands, or ears.

Certified reflexologist Helen Chin Lui of the Healing Center in Medford, Massachusetts, says that each ear contains a complete reflex map of the body, rich with nerve endings and multiple connectors to the central nervous system.

Here are some ways to relieve pain by applying pressure to specific parts of your ears.

• The uppermost portion of your ear is associated with your back and shoulders. Fastening a clothespin or applying pressure with your fingers to this part of your ear for about a minute several times a day should reduce built-up tension and lessen your back and shoulder pain.

• A little further down your ear is a spot associated with your body's internal organs. Apply pressure in a similar way here to reduce minor internal discomfort.

• The upper-middle part of your ear is associated with your joints. Applying pressure here with a clothespin or your fingers can offer relief from joint pain and stiffness.

• The lower-middle part of your ear is associated with your sinuses and throat. When seeking relief from a cold or sinus infection, applying pressure to this spot can reduce sinus tension and throat soreness.

• Just above the lobe of your ear is a spot most commonly associated with digestion. Using a clothespin here to apply pressure can help relieve digestive issues and minor stomach problems. If you often feel digestive discomfort, you also can use this method in advance as a preventative.

• The lowest part of your ear—your lobe—is the spot associated with your head and heart. Applying pressure to your earlobe can relieve unwanted pressure in your head and can effectively eliminate pressure headaches.

THE POWER OF SPICES AND HERBS

	What It Can Do	What You Can Do
Basil	Uplift your spirits and relieve headaches and migraines	Add basil to your recipes or apply a few drops of basil oil to a tissue and inhale
Caraway	Quiet a cough and relieve gas	Add one teaspoon of caraway seed to omelets or toast, or steep two tablespoons in two cups boiling water for 10 minutes. Strain, sweeten with honey, and drink hot
Cloves	Protect teeth and gums by inhibiting the growth of oral bacteria Kill germs and help destroy E. coli in contaminated meat	Sprinkle one teaspoon of ground cloves per pound of meat before cooking, or add one or two cloves to a cup of tea.
Cumin	Prevent strokes. Cumin inhibits thromboxane, a compound that stimulates blood platelet aggregation. Preventing platelets from sticking together may help prevent the blood clots that lead to strokes and heart attacks	Sprinkle ground cumin seeds on salads, Mexican dishes, or Indian dishes
Ginger	Ease aches and pains. Gingerols, the active compounds in ginger, inhibit cyclooxygenase, the enzyme that induces inflammation Relieve nausea and motion sickness	Add one-third teaspoon of ground ginger to a cup of hot tea, or drink a cup of ginger tea. Add one-half teaspoon to desserts, or eat a piece of ginger candy

The Power of Spices and Herbs, continued...

	What It Can Do	What You Can Do
Fennel	Relieve hay fever. Fennel is rich in quercetin, a flavonoid that stabilizes the body's histamine-releasing mast cells to boost their resistance to allergens. Relieve GI distress. One serving of fennel a day can soothe bellyaches, bloating, and indigestion by 65 percent. Relieve or prevent bruise marks, because of fennel's antioxidant flavonoid, rutin. Fennel also can accelerate recovery from cuts and scrapes, because of its antimicrobial kaempferol.	Add thinly sliced or chopped fennel to salads, sauces, and soups
Turmeric	Improve memory. Curcumin, a compound in turmeric, helps ward off mental decline. A diet rich in curcumin reduces the buildup of beta-amyloid, a plaquelike substance that affects memory by blocking communication between brain cells. Decrease body fat Heal cuts and scrapes	Mix one-quarter teaspoon of turmeric with vegetables. Aim for a total of one tablespoon turmeric daily. For a wound, mix two tablespoons of turmeric powder, one teaspoon lemon juice, and just enough water to make a smooth paste to spread over a cleansed wound

EASE PREMENSTRUAL SYNDROME (PMS)

- Drink more fluids. You may feel bloated, but continue to drink eight glasses of plain water each day of your period.

- Exercise. Stretching at the end of the day will relieve cramps.

- Include calcium in your diet and take magnesium to reduce PMS-related water retention by more than a third.

- Beverages containing caffeine and alcohol have a diuretic effect, and several other foods including celery, onion, eggplant, asparagus, and watermelon are said to increase urine output, as well. In natural medicine, the herbs hawthorn, corn silk, and parsley are used as diuretics, too. Of these, hawthorn (*Crataegus oxycanthus*) is the most powerful.

- Add cinnamon to your diet to decrease cramps.

- Take vitamin E, two doses of 200 IU daily, two days before and three days into your period, to decrease pain intensity and blood loss.

TAKE YOUR VITAMINS AND MINERALS

- Pumpkin seeds are a good source of vitamin E, copper, and magnesium.

- For cooking vegetables, steaming is better than boiling, as boiling can break down vitamins.

- A supplement regimen containing adequate amounts of both calcium and vitamin D can help prevent osteoporosis.

- Getting 400 mcg a day of folate can prevent heart disease. If you are of childbearing age, know that taking folate can cut in half the incidence of brain and spinal cord birth defects in babies. Folate can be found in green leafy vegetables, sunflower seeds, peanuts, edamame, and liver.

- The tables on the following pages include the Institute of Medicine of the National Academies Food and Nutrition Board's recommended dosages of vitamins and minerals for adults aged 19 to 50.

PREVENT ACCIDENTS

- To avoid burning your fingers, use a match to light a stick of spaghetti, and then use that to light hard-to-reach candlewicks.

- To avoid hitting your fingers, use a clothespin to hold a nail while hammering.

- Avoid bites from mosquitoes and bugs by using these tips.
    o For a pest-free picnic table, add five drops of lavender essential oil to 32 ounces of water. Pour into a spray bottle to spritz and wipe down your table and chairs.
    o To prevent mosquitoes from biting you while you sleep, dab a little citronella oil on your bed's headboard.
    o For a bug-free room, put a couple of drops of lavender or peppermint essential oil on a cool lightbulb of a lamp to help repel insects when you turn it on.

o Aim a fan at a doorway, blowing out. Flies are very sensitive to air currents and generally will not travel through moving air.

o Mix two drops of oil of peppermint or lavender with two teaspoons of almond or sweet oil and dab on your skin for a natural insect repellent.

o If you are susceptible to mosquito bites (as I am), take one vitamin B1 tablet (Thiamine Hydrochloride 100 mg) a day from April through October. Although you cannot smell it, the odor the ingested tablet gives out through your skin repels mosquitoes and some other biting bugs. However, it does not seem to work on stinging insects.

• Input your In Case of Emergency (ICE) phone numbers in your cell phone. Choose the numbers of two people to be notified in case of an emergency, such as those who know your current allergies and medications. Name their entries in your directory as "ICE Mom" or "ICE Husband," for example. If you are involved in an emergency with another person, do not forget to check that person's cell phone to see if he or she has programmed an ICE number.

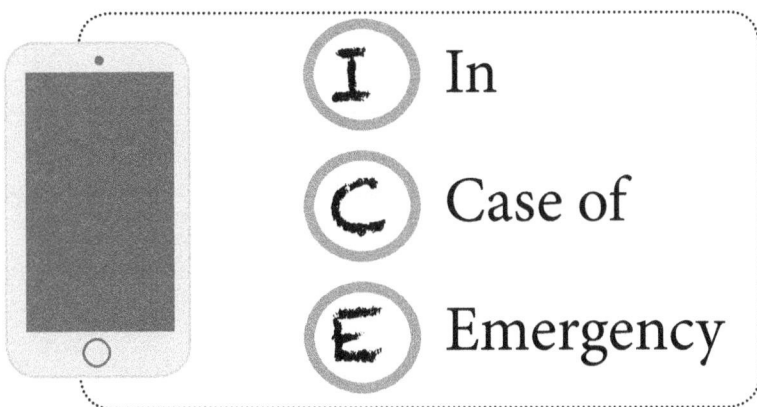

RECOMMENDED DOSAGES OF VITAMINS FOR ADULTS AGED 19 TO 50

Vitamin	Helps Support	Daily Require-ment	Common Natural Sources
Vitamin A	Eyes	5,000 IU 700 mcg	Butter, cod liver oil, egg yolks, liver, milk
Vitamin B1 (Thiamine)	Energy	10-50 mcg	Brown rice, eggs, legumes, oatmeal, oranges, pasta, peanuts, pork , watermelon, wheat germ
Vitamin B2 (Riboflavin)	Eyes, cell devel-opment	10-50 mcg	Asparagus, avocados, beef, broccoli, cottage cheese, milk, mushrooms, prunes, salmon, tangerines, turkey
Vitamin B3 (Niacin)	Fat, protein and carbohy-drate metab-olism, nervous system	25 mg (more in supplement form with medical su-pervision)	Asparagus, baked potatoes, broccoli, fish, legumes, meats, peanut butter, poultry, soybeans, whole grains
Vitamin B6	Brain, heart, immune system, protein metabolism	50-200 mg	Avocados, bananas, cauliflower, chicken, fish, green peppers, lima beans, potatoes, raisins, soybeans, spinach
Vitamin B12	Nerves, blood, tissue growth	50-100 mcg	Cheese, clams, eggs, mussels, oysters, salmon, swordfish, tuna
Vitamin C	Immune sys-tem	1,000-2,000 mg	Bell peppers, broccoli, cabbage, citrus fruit, kiwifruit, melons, raspberries, spinach, strawberries, tomatoes
Vitamin D	Bones, calcium absorption	1,000-2,000 IU 25-50 mg	Sunlight, eggs, milk, salmon, tuna
Vitamin E	Heart, immune system	200-400 IU 15 mg	Apples, blackberries, broccoli, mangoes, nut and vegetable oils, peanuts, pumpkin seeds, spinach, wheat germ, whole wheat
Vitamin K	Blood clotting	90 mcg	Avocados, broccoli, brussels sprouts, cabbage, carrots, dairy products, eggs, parsley, spinach, tomatoes

RECOMMENDED DOSAGES OF MINERALS
FOR ADULTS AGED 19 TO 50

Mineral	Helps Support	Daily Requirement	Common Natural Sources
Beta carotene and other mixed carotenoids	Immune system	5,000-15,000 IU	Apricots, broccoli, butternut squash, cantaloupe, carrots, mangoes, pumpkin, spinach, sweet potatoes, tuna, watermelon
Iron	Oxygen in blood, energy, metabolism	15-20 mg (8 mg for women over 50)	Asparagus, chicken, clams, meats, prunes, pumpkin seeds, raisins, soybeans, spinach, tofu
Magnesium	Blood pressure, energy, nerve and muscle function	400-600 mg	Baked potatoes, bananas, broccoli, dairy products, molasses, nuts, pumpkin seeds, seafood, spinach, wheat germ
Manganese	Blood sugar, energy	2-10 mg	Dried fruits, green leafy vegetables, legumes, nuts, spinach, whole grains
Molybdenum	Energy, metabolism	25-250 mcg	Dairy products, legumes, meats, whole grains
Omega-3	Brain and memory support, cholesterol	400 mg	Flaxseeds, salmon, soybeans, walnuts
Pantothenic Acid	Energy, metabolism	25-150 mg	Avocados, broccoli, cashews, eggs, fish, lentils, mushrooms, peanuts, soybeans, whole grains
Phosphorus	Energy, bones (teams up with calcium)	800-1,000 mg	Dairy products, eggs, fish, meats, poultry

RECOMMENDED DOSAGES OF MINERALS
FOR ADULTS AGED 19 TO 50, CONTINUED...

Mineral	Helps Support	Daily Requirement	Common Natural Sources
Potassium	Acid balance in body, fluid balance (works with sodium)	4,700-6,000 mg (from food sources)	Avocados, bananas, cantaloupe, milk, mushrooms, potatoes, spinach, tomatoes, yogurt
Selenium	Immune system	100-300 mcg	Brazil nuts, dairy products, fish, meats, mushrooms, shellfish, whole grains
Sodium	Fluid balance, nervous system function	400 mg	Processed food, salt, soy sauce. Note: Most people will not have to supplement their sodium intake due to their high salt intake
Zinc	Immune system, prostate, wound healing	8-40 mg	Dairy products, lean beef, legumes, lima beans, nuts, oysters, poultry, seafood, wheat germ

<u>WORRY LESS</u>

Worried about an uncomfortable or unsettling symptom? For
90 percent of women, the real causes of common yet frightening
symptoms are benign. Below are some examples.

<u>MANAGING BENIGN SYMPTOMS OF STRESS</u>

Symptom	It Might Mean This	Try This To See If It Helps
Memory lapses	Reduced sensitivity to insulin, the hormone that shuttles blood sugar to body cells	Add a few drops of cinnamon extract or one teaspoon of powered cinnamon to your diet
Increased bruising	Vitamin C deficiency	Make sure to get 1,000 mg of vitamin C daily.
Body-wide pain	Sinusitis	Hot showers and inhaling steamy air for 15 minutes each day can reduce sinus inflammation and ease related body pain within 72 hours
Shaky Hands	Magnesium deficiency	Eat at least two servings daily of magnesium-rich foods, such as nuts, pumpkin and sunflower seeds, tofu, and leafy greens. Make sure you are getting 400 to 600 mg of magnesium a day

Chapter Six
Improve Your Memory

On my mother's kitchen cabinet was a cartoon of two dinosaurs on the shore looking out on Noah's Ark. One dinosaur says to the other, "Are you kidding? That was today?" As much as it amused me, it also provided a stark reminder of the importance of remembering things.

My sister-in-law, Judie, is eight years older than I am and has the best memory I have ever encountered. She can remember what each of us had for dinner at which restaurant on a visit 10 years ago. One evening, she called about my mother-in-law, who at the time was in her late 70s. "Val, I am really worried about Mom," she said. "Guess what she did? Last night, she went up the stairs and when she got to the top, she asked, 'Why did I come up here?' She totally forgot why she went upstairs!"

I laughed and replied. "Are you kidding me?"

"No, I am not kidding," she answered. "I am really worried about her."

Still laughing, I said, "I do that a couple times a day!"

She then said, "Well, listen to this. This is what worries me even more. Last week, Mom came out of the store and could not remember where she parked her car."

I responded, "Again, are you kidding me? Thank God for the button on my keychain to make my car beep so I can find it."

Truth be told, for a while before that conversation with Judie, I had been worrying about my own memory lapses, similar to the ones she described. When I expressed my concerns to my doctor, she said, "If you forget where you put your keys, that is okay. Now, if you forget what your keys are used for, then come and talk to me." She also recommended that it would be a good exercise to research what is "normal" forgetfulness, to put things into perspective and find out what I could do to improve my memory. So I did. Here are some of the things I found out.

> *Memory lapses are normal. Our minds are designed to forget.*

Memory lapses are normal. Our minds are designed to forget. After all, if we remembered every place we ever parked our cars or everything we ate, our brains would be too cluttered to access things that are important. It is normal to lose more than half of the information that enters your head within an hour and 80 percent within a month.

DEAL WITH COMMON MEMORY LAPSES

- *"Why am I here?"* Have you ever gotten to the top of the stairs and wondered why you came up? To recover your memory, think back to what you were thinking when you started up the stairs. If this fails, actually walk back to the place where you started. This often will bring your last thought back to you. Check out what you are carrying to remind yourself of what you were planning to do. If you are carrying a hanger, you might have been setting out to retrieve a piece of clothing.

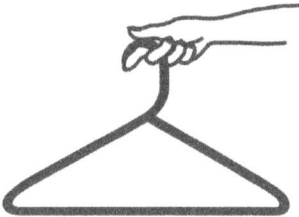

If you are holding an envelope, you might have been looking for a stamp.

- *"What is her name?"* I frequently say, "I know that I have met you before, but I am sorry, I have forgotten your name. I am Valerie Roman. Would you please tell me your name again?" There is a good chance that the person also has forgotten your name and will appreciate the reintroduction. To remember a name you have just heard, repeat it aloud by saying, "Nice to meet you, Mary" or "What a distinguished name Humphrey is!" Make a connection between the name and other information you already know. For example, "I had a friend in college named Valerie" or "Valerie, do you spell that with an ie or a y?" Thinking of alliterative descriptions of the person, such as "Skinny Susan" or "Balding Bob," can help. At conventions and reunions when you meet many people at once, put the names to paper and read what you have written before bed. Writing them down provides your brain with another route to recall.

- *"Where did I put my keys?"* Train yourself to put keys and glasses in the same spot every time. Do not leave them in pockets, and make sure that teenage children always remember to return keys to their designated place (a certain wall hook or tabletop dish?) every time!

- *"How can I find that place?"* Most people can only remember the first two steps in a set of driving directions. Try the Roman Room Method (no, not named after me). Picture your bedroom or any other familiar room in your house and link driving directions to your movements in that room. For example, "Turn right and go through three lights" might translate to "Pivot right at the sock drawer and pull out three socks."

- *"Where did I park?"* When you walk away from your car, turn around and look at the location to lock a visual image of it in your mind. Lampposts, trees, and puddles give you visual markers that will help you remember. To ensure that I can find my car in an unmarked lot, I always try to park in the row that directly leads to the door, no matter how far back I need to go. Of course, I always have my keychain with the beeper button in hand.

MIND YOUR MIND

- Make up a silly story when trying to remember a list of words. For example, let us say you have to remember these words: vase, door, monkey, clouds, gift, and brownies. Your story could be: "There was a vase that walked out the door and saw a monkey. The monkey looked up at the clouds and saw a boxed gift floating in the air. The box fell and it was filled with brownies." The sillier the story, the better you will remember it.

- Count the items that you are taking when you are going somewhere. For example, your coat, scarf, hat, purse, and umbrella would total five. Before returning home, make sure you have the five items.

- Each time you think about something you need to do or get, record a reminder to yourself. Most smartphones have a voice recording option; otherwise, call home and leave yourself a message. A lot of our memory battle—and stress about it—is worrying about how to remember what we have just thought. If you record it, you know that you have captured it and can just listen to your recording later.

- Keep track of when you are due for annual medical checks, such as your mammogram, Pap smear, annual physical, and colonoscopy, by creating a Word or spreadsheet document.

- Stay friendly. People who have an active social life may have a slower rate of memory decline.

- Exercise. Exercise improves attention, memory, accuracy, and how quickly you process information—all of which helps you make smarter decisions. Exercising with others, whether in a class or playing a game, sharpens your memory even more.

- Take up dancing. Cardiovascular health is more important than any other factor in preserving and improving memory. Twenty minutes of physical activity per day can markedly decrease memory deterioration. Dancing combines physical activity with social interaction, the ideal combination for enhancing memory.

- Do mental gymnastics, such as crossword puzzles and Sudoku. Regular mental challenges cut the risk of dementia nearly in half.

- Playing an instrument is an excellent way to keep your mind in working order. The combination of mental and physical effort increases your coordination and concentration.

- Take a break. Studies show that not only is a nice cup of coffee in the afternoon a welcome change of pace, but it also may improve your memory. Also, just taking a break helps. As the Brits say, "A change is as good as a rest."

- Get enough sleep. There is evidence that sleeping enhances memory, and that a 45-minute afternoon nap can restore alertness and help with long-term memory formation. The Europeans seem to understand this. Wouldn't it be nice if the U.S. instituted siestas!

- Eat right. Some of the key foods for memory support include almonds and walnuts (vitamin E), blueberries and citrus fruits (vitamin C), fortified grains (folic acid, vitamin B), and green leafy vegetables and fish (omega-3 fatty acids).

- Take gingko biloba, an herb that many researchers say can improve and protect memory. Also take pycnogenol, an antioxidant derived from tree bark that has been shown to improve memory in the elderly. You just need to remember to take these herbs on a regular basis! And, as with all herbal supplements, you should consult your physician before taking them.

- Chew gum. People who chewed gum for 20 minutes performed 35 percent better on memory tests. Chewing stimulates your brain's temporal lobe, which contains the memory-storing hippocampus. The act of chewing, in other words, wakes us up, ensuring that we are fully focused on the task at hand. People chewing mint gum showed a dramatic decrease in feelings of sleepiness.

- If you believe that you can remember something, you actually have a better chance of remembering it. If you want to remember something, say to yourself, "Remember this: The umbrella is in the hall closet." Attitude makes a difference. Adults who believe they have a bad memory are more forgetful than those who do not.

- Try to control your stress level (yeah, right). People who are chronically stressed are more likely to develop cognitive impairment. Cortisol, the hormone produced in times of stress, interferes with memory, as well as creates belly fat. So maybe relaxed deep breathing while running around trying to find your keys may help you find them next time!

Chapter Seven
The Hunt for Happiness

I n September 2009, Tony and I went on a 15-day tour to Greece. There were 37 people on the tour from various places in the United States. Being of Greek descent, I was asked if we had the "Big Fat Greek Wedding," like in the movie by that name, to which Tony immediately responded, "Sure did!" Indeed, we had about 200 people on my side of the church and 20 on his! One woman on the trip asked if I knew Greek dances. I responded that I did and that I would be happy to teach her if she was interested. I had taught Greek dancing to Tony and our wedding party of 14, which included seven klutzy ushers, so I was confident I could teach it to anyone. To my surprise, the tour guide announced, "Val's Greek Dancing Lessons outside by the hotel pool at 6 p.m." These lessons became an official social event—appearing on the official tour poster!

About an hour from start time, I went down to the pool to work with the bartender to pull the music together. I began to notice that sitting on one side of the pool were all my fellow American tour travelers; on another side were about 20 to 30 middle-age to elderly native Greeks; and on another side were about a dozen tourists from Norway who we had met at dinner the night before. When I looked up, I saw guests standing out on their room balconies to view the event. I jokingly asked the tour guide, "Did you tell the whole hotel and town about this?"

She laughed and said, "Not really, but the hotel owners were very excited about the idea, so I think they may have advertised it."

Here I was, in the spotlight. I was not nervous, since I truly enjoy teaching Greek dancing. The shy Americans in our group, who said that they never danced, watched from their seats. The Greeks and the Norwegians did, too. The Greeks appeared to be a bit skeptical, with their strong, stoic faces. After all, who was this American woman teaching their native dances? The Norwegians also seemed to be uncertain about what was happening. But my lesson went really well, and within 15 minutes, my students and I were all dancing around the pool.

As I traveled past the somewhat guarded and weary-looking Greeks, I decided to "go for it." I asked some of them, in Greek, if they would please dance with us. I said, "You know these dances better than any of us, so please join in."

At first I received "No, no" and shake-of-the-head responses. But I became a bit more daring my next time past them; I put my hand out and again pleaded for them to share in the fun.

One Greek woman joined us, and finally with some additional prodding, a Greek man did, too. Before I knew it, the Greeks were dancing with the Americans, who were dancing with the Norwegians, who were dancing with the Greeks. Everyone was smiling. Even the people who said they had never danced before were out there dancing around the pool, as well as our very shy tour bus driver.

People continued to dance even after dinner was announced. An old Greek woman continued to dance for over an hour, grinning from ear to ear, frequently bellowing the traditional Greek "Opa! Opa!" This is the Greeks' way of describing jubilance, their way of expressing that they feel serenely exuberant and able to enjoy life like children do. The elderly Greek woman later told me in Greek, "Honey, I have not danced in over 20 years. You are my granddaughter—I love you." My heart melted. The event was a success.

I was continually thanked by my fellow travelers, as well as by the owners and guests of the hotel, for the wonderful time I had given them that night. I relished the fact that I had had a positive impact on their lives. They would remember that evening forever. In fact, one person said, "Hillary Clinton, watch out!" after witnessing the improvement I had wrought in international relations!

> *Happiness comes from within. If you think you are happy, you are happy.*

What is the secret to happiness? This is the subject that I have explored the most. David Burns's book *Feeling Good* (my personal favorite), Marci Shimoff's *Happy for No Reason*, Eckhart Tolle's *A New Earth* (personally a tough read for me), and Rhonda Byrne's *The Secret* are just a few excellent books about happiness. The sad fact is that about a quarter of American adults are clinically depressed. Depression is the leading cause of disability worldwide. Doctors predict that depression will be the second largest global burden of illness, right behind heart disease, in just a few years.

The secret to happiness may still be a secret, but one thing I have learned is that happiness is not provided to you. You need to make your own. Happiness comes from within. If you think you are happy, you are happy.

Through reading and through other experiences, here is what I have learned about how to feel happy.

<u>HELP YOUR BODY FEEL HAPPY</u>

- Eat foods with omega-3 fatty acids to fight depression and memory problems. Avoid omega-6 fatty acids, since they counteract the benefits of omega-3 fatty acids.

- Eat blueberries. The antioxidants in blueberries can improve your mood and help you focus.

- Include folic acid and the vitamin B in your diet. They have been linked with the brain functions that prevent depression and memory loss.

- To increase your level of serotonin, the chemical that improves mood, eat more carbohydrates than protein and fat. Increasing your serotonin level is what antidepressants, such as Zoloft, Prozac, and Paxil, are designed to do. Judith Wurtman, author of *The Serotonin Power Diet*, advocates a carbohydrate-rich diet and recommends that women eat pretzels, crackers, popcorn, or any other high-carbohydrate snack around 4 p.m. to boost their serotonin and energy levels.

- Eat right. Julia Ross, author of the books *The Mood Cure* and *The Diet Cure*, believes that much of our ability to be happy depends upon meeting our nutritional needs. According to Ross, your body has four key happiness-producing neurotransmitters that are fueled by amino acids. If your amino acid levels are sufficient and the four neurotransmitter levels are high, then you will generally feel happy and positive. Your four key neurotransmitters are endorphins, gamma-aminobutyric acid (GABA), catecholamines (norepinephrine, adrenalin, and dopamine), and serotonin. The following chart explains. More information can be found at www.moodcure.com.

FOUR NEUROTRANSMITTERS CONTRIBUTING TO HAPPINESS &
THEIR RELATED AMINO ACIDS

Neurotrans-mitter	If Level Is High	If Level Is Low	Related Amino Acids
Endorphins	Comfort-able, happy	Overly sensitive, cry easily	DL-phenylalanine D-phenylalanine
GABA	Relaxed, stress-free	Over-whelmed, stressed, tensed muscles	GABA L-taurine
Catecholamines	Alert, full of energy	Lethargic, feel blah, tired	L-tyrosine L-phenylalanine
Serotonin	Positive, confident, easygoing	Worried, irritable, sleepless	5-HTP Melatonin

• Be conscious of your body's cycles. A woman's three major reproductive hormones—estrogen, progesterone, and testosterone—play a major role in how she feels. During the first week of the menstrual cycle, the levels of all three hormones are low. The low levels reduce the output of the brain's mood-elevating neuropeptides, such as serotonin. This is when most women feel blue. Instead of denying that you feel lousy, treat yourself to a night out with friends, a movie, a facial, or a massage. Understanding the blues just before and during the menstrual period helps women manage their mood swings. During the second week of your cycle, estrogen and testosterone are high and progesterone is still low. Your mood-elevating norepinephrine and dopamine rise, so this is a time of energy, brighter moods, and confidence. It is an ideal time to take on new challenges or work on new ideas. During the third and most of the fourth week of your cycle, your progesterone level is high, increasing your ability to be calm and clearheaded and offering a great time to be reflective. During the last few days of your cycle, the level of all three hormones is low, returning to what they were during your first week.

<u>TAKE ACTION TO BE HAPPY</u>

- Do good things for others and give more than you take. The positive psychological effect of doing any type of good deed or community service is that it truly boosts your mood. Donate blood, volunteer time (something I know you have a lot of ☺) to a local senior center or food kitchen, or help someone carry groceries from the store to the car. Doing a few good deeds each week can significantly boost your spirits.

- Be compassionate. The Dalai Lama once said, "If you want others to be happy, practice compassion; if you want to be happy, practice compassion."

- Give thanks and appreciate what you have. People who describe themselves as feeling grateful have more energy and optimism and suffer less stress and clinical depression than the population as a whole. Those who regularly practice gratitude can enhance their natural set point for happiness by as much as 25 percent, reports Robert Emmons, PhD, in his book, *Thanks! How Practicing Gratitude Can Make You Happier*. Through his research, Dr. Emmons found that people who kept gratitude journals felt better about their lives, exercised more, and were more optimistic.

- Keep a "Thankful Diary." Each evening before going to bed, list two or three things for which you are grateful. For example, "My husband and children" or "My lifelong friend, Gail" or "My relationships with my friend, Melinda, and my cousin, Kathie." Each morning, read your list. Repeat that routine each evening and morning. The French novelist Sidonie-Gabrielle Colette, best known for her novel *Gigi*, once said, "What a wonderful life I have had. I only wish I had realized it sooner."

- Do not be judgmental. Accept other people as they are.

- Make people a priority in your life.

- Choose to believe that the universe is here to support you, not that it is out to get you. When something bad happens, instead of moping or saying "Why me?" think of it as, "This is happening for my own good. I do not see why yet, but it will become evident later on." Decide to have faith that every event ultimately contains a lesson or gift. Remember the story of the farmer whose horse ran away? His friends felt sorry for his bad luck. He replied, "Bad luck? Good luck? Who knows?" A few days later, the horse returned with 10 other wild horses, and his friends congratulated him on his good luck. He replied, "Good luck? Bad luck? Who knows?" Later that week, while his son was trying to train one of the wild horses, he fell off and broke his leg. His friends said they were sorry for his bad luck. Again, the farmer responded, "Bad luck? Good luck? Who knows?" A week later, the army came to draft all the young men.

"Good luck? Bad luck? Who knows?"

However, when they saw that the farmer's son had broken his leg, they let him stay. So, good luck or bad luck? You never know.

- Let others know how much they mean to you. When I was 40 years old, I wrote a letter to my high school English teacher, Sheila Segal, to let her know how powerful an impact she had had on my life. It meant a lot to her and to me. We have continued to keep in touch and have developed a wonderfully special friendship.

- Practice happiness. Thomas Jefferson wrote that we all have the right to life, liberty, and the pursuit of happiness. He used the word "pursuit" to mean to practice an activity, to do it regularly, and to make a habit of it. Laughing, meditating, and spending time with people I care about are just a few of the activities that I practice regularly and have become habits. Life is too short, so I try to spend it with people who make me laugh and make me happy. It took me a long time to learn to stop chasing after happiness and start practicing it, instead.

- Smile as soon as you wake up, to create a happy setting that your brain can easily revisit.

- Rid yourself of guilt. Is guilt or regret about something getting to you? Try the Bio-Energetic Synchronization Technique (B.E.S.T.), developed by Dr. M. T. Morter, Jr., and described at the website www.morter.com. One exercise is called the M-Power March: Make Peace with Yourself. This is how it is done:
    1. Stand up straight in a comfortable and relaxed position, arms at your sides.
    2. Step your left foot out, slightly bending your left knee. Keep your right foot in place.

3. Raise your right arm to a 45-degree angle in front of you and extend your left arm behind you to a 45-degree angle.
4. Turn your head to your right, close your eyes, and stretch your neck. Think of something that you feel guilty about. Take a deep breath and focus on feeling forgiveness. Hold your breath and this position for 10 seconds.
5. Exhale and repeat the position with your opposite leg and arm.
6. Repeat three times.

THINK YOURSELF TO HAPPINESS

- Depression may be a failure to appreciate positive experiences. Depressed people were not nearly as successful at learning positive information as their nondepressed counterparts.

- Get outside yourself. The more self-absorbed you are, the more your world closes in; the more your world closes in, the less realistic you become and the more oblivious you are to the needs of others. Caring for others can break this vicious cycle. It is true that it is more blessed to give than to receive. Think about monkeys at the zoo picking the bugs out of each other's fur. Primates groom each other after a stressful event and experience a reduction in blood pressure.

- Embrace suffering as an opportunity to learn. Everyone has problems. Consider them feedback, not failures.

- Avoid dwelling in the past or worrying about the future. Worrying will not take away tomorrow's problems; it only takes away today's peace. Live in the moment.

- Drop the need to impress others or seek their approval.

- Let go of the need to be always right. Counting to 10 before you correct someone or biting your tongue before you come up with your "better way" will help you break the habit of having the last word. It is an important life skill to recognize that a job can be completed without your expert help!

- Do not play the blame game. Instead of looking back to see whose fault it was, look forward. Looking ahead to find a solution will endear you to others, as well as save time. Some successful people have mastered saying the statement "It may have been my fault" even when it clearly was not, in order to move the group forward towards a solution.

- Throw out the myth of "I will be happy when . . . ," such as, "I will be happy when I lose 10 pounds" or "I will be happy when I get a promotion or "I will be happy when the kids are older." Instead, be glad that you are eating right and are on your way to losing 10 pounds, that you are learning your job and may get a promotion, or that your kids are growing up to be good people and you can see that already. With this way of thinking, happiness actually can be experienced right now in this very moment.

- Maintain a good sense of humor. A sense of humor can cut a cancer patient's chance of premature death by 70 percent and can add years to your life. Cultivate your sense of humor by watching clips on YouTube and comedy specials on HBO or by reading books by humorists, such as David Sedaris and Erma Bombeck. Once you learn to make a joke of things, you will be able to find the fun in life's setbacks.

- Choose to be happy. You have a choice in how you look at things. I have often said to myself that "stressed" is a bad word, but if you look at it from a different perspective—backward in this case—"desserts" seem pretty good. As Eleanor Roosevelt once said, "No one can make you feel inferior without your consent." Never put the keys to your happiness in someone else's pocket. Learn to appreciate yourself and expect others to do the same.

- The Greek philosopher, Epictetus, said, "We are disturbed not by what happens to us, but by our thoughts about what happens." How true! Try to turn off the dire predictions and insulting assessments that you are manufacturing about yourself. When you find yourself expecting the worst, try reciting a poem or saying a prayer to push negative thoughts off your brain's center stage.

- Do not be shy about acknowledging kudos from others. Most women are comfortable encouraging the work of others, but not welcoming praise themselves. Many people like giving accolades, so when they come your way, accept them with pleasure and gratitude. I learned this for myself when I applied through the Twelve College Exchange program to spend my junior year on another college campus. I received two acceptance letters: one from Dartmouth College applauding my choice in applying there because of its world-class facilities, and one from Bowdoin College commenting on what an addition I would make to its community. I accepted Bowdoin's offer because I felt they appreciated me. I have never regretted that choice.

GOAL TWO

HAVE A GREAT CAREER

.

Goal Two
Have A Great Career

B ecause of the goals my parents instilled in me, I was driven to achieve. I graduated as the valedictorian from my high school and graduated Phi Beta Kappa from Wellesley College, majoring in math, economics, and secondary school education. My parents were so proud, and their pride was all I really needed during those years.

During my senior year at Wellesley, I was not sure what I wanted to do after graduation. I could have become a math teacher in a local high school, something that I had dreamed about from the age of eight. However, right or wrong, I had learned at Wellesley College that I should be more enterprising and seek an occupation not traditionally filled by women.

In the 1970s, there were no computer science degrees. In fact, there were no computer courses offered at Wellesley. But one day in the spring term, my last semester of college, I saw a notice that the U.S. Census Bureau was coming to campus to recruit new employees. President John F. Kennedy had inspired me (and many others of my generation) to serve our country, so the prospect of working for the federal government was very appealing. I signed up for an interview.

Two weeks later, I was offered the opportunity to move to Washington, D.C., that summer to learn computer programming at the government's expense. After racking up so many student loans during the previous four years, I was thrilled they actually were going to pay me to learn new skills. And I had always lived in New England, so although a bit daunting, the idea of experiencing another part of the country was alluring.

Three weeks after graduating from Wellesley, I moved to Washington to start my career in computers. I took my first full-time job as a junior programmer. I told myself I would go to D.C. for one year, but ended up staying there for seven years. During my time there, I was fortunate to have great supervisors and mentors. I climbed the career ladder quickly and before long, became the director of systems analysis and design. My job at the Census Bureau was the keystone to my long and happy career.

My career has always been very important to me, but so has my family, and I have been very fortunate that each career move in my life has balanced both needs. I left the programming job in Washington not only to become the first technology director ever for the City of Cambridge, Massachusetts, but also to bring my children closer to their grandparents. Finally, after 11 years working for the City of Cambridge, I took the job as director of technology at the esteemed preparatory high school Phillips Academy in Andover, Massachusetts. I switched to the Academy not only to have the chance to positively impact young people's lives in an educational setting, but also to cut my commute in half and to provide my sons the

opportunity to attend there. Some say that you cannot have a successful career and be a good mother. I disagree. Everything can be intertwined.

There is no doubt that balancing career and home life is challenging. Juggling different roles is difficult, and I have constantly needed to figure out ways to succeed in a male-dominated career, handle stress, manage my time, and be organized whether I was in the office, in the kitchen, at a school conference, or on the soccer field.

Chapter Eight
Women and the Workplace

I have worked full time professionally all my adult life, with the exceptions of a six-month break after giving birth to my first child and a three-month break after giving birth to my second child. Whether I was at the Census Bureau, at the City of Cambridge, or at Phillips Academy, I had long, stress-filled workdays that came with long commutes in rush-hour traffic. Every job has positives and negatives, but focusing on the positives is important in pushing through the hardships and finding each job more fulfilling in its own way. I am proud that I was able to make inroads for women in a male-dominated field. I was five feet tall in a world of six footers. It was difficult, but one of the perks was that I never had to wait in line for the ladies' room!

Working for the federal government in the Jimmy Carter and Ronald Reagan administrations was wonderful for a young woman. The government was well ahead of the curve of political correctness. I learned words such as "chair" instead of "chairman" and "staff resources" instead of "manpower." I was treated equally and was provided numerous training opportunities not only in technical training, but in management training as well. The concept of a woman manager seemed very natural there, and I had many women as role models and colleagues. That prepared me so well for my next opportunity, to be the first technology director for the City of Cambridge.

Cambridge is a great city. It is the home of Harvard and the Massachusetts Institute of Technology (MIT) and is affectionately called "The People's Republic of Cambridge," because of its progressive perspectives. I discovered, however, that while its colleges and many of its citizens were progressive, that was not the case for the city administration itself. The administration was an old boys' network, which was very different from what I had experienced in Washington. Most power positions—such as city manager, assistant city manager, finance director, human resources director, and budget director—were filled by men. Most were married to women who were stay-at-home mothers. Fortunately, however, my direct supervisor, the finance director, was married to a woman who was a very successful financial executive. So he was empathetic to me and confident enough to be able to take in stride the sexist comments of the time, such as, "You know who wears the pants in that family" or "You better ask his wife if he can go."

I made two other inroads during my 11-year tenure at the City of Cambridge. Aside from being the first female technology director, I also was the first woman to participate in the office football pools. When I initially asked to join, one man joked, "What are you going to do, pick the teams by the color of their uniforms?" I had not worked there long, so he had no idea that I was, and have always been, a very big sports fan. Not many of the men were happy yet to have a female head of department, and they definitely were not happy when I also beat them in the football pool!

The other inroad occurred three years later, when I became pregnant with my second child. Now this was a dilemma. Because, as I was told, I was the "first woman department head of childbearing age," we would need to break new ground to establish guidelines on how to manage a department in absentia. Nowadays, the idea of naming an acting director is fairly common, but it was not an option back then. So I worked from home for three months and then part-time for three months. We all survived the experience without a hitch, just as I had expected.

In the third and last leg of my career, I served as the director of technology at Phillips Academy for 13 years. It was as if I had taken a 180-degree turn. Many of the top power positions at Phillips Academy—head of school, assistant head of school, dean of admission, and human resources director—were filled by women. Again, I was blessed with many role models and mentors.

As a female manager at all three of my jobs, I tried to make the best use of the strengths of being a woman. My intuition, listening skills, strong moral beliefs, and genuine caring about people and their professional development allowed me to realize my career-long success in hiring and retaining high-quality employees. I built productive teams by creating work environments that fostered individual employee growth. I gained a reputation with supervisors and subordinates as a good manager. Early in my career, I attended a seminar that required us to write down a list of five people who had most influenced, supported, and impacted our lives. Of course, I listed my parents. I also listed Sheila Segal, my high school teacher, and Bob Munsey, who supervised and mentored me at the Census Bureau. And I listed Gail Printy, my friend now of more than 50 years.

After we completed our lists, we were asked, "Now think about people who you manage. Would any of them put you on their lists?" From that moment on, I have focused on having a positive and lasting effect on other people's lives. I have told this story to several people, and it has brought me such happiness when many have written to me, "You are on my list."

To get ahead, women do not need to get into the "I need to be more aggressive" or the "Only some of us make it, so we must knock down other women" syndromes. It is so infuriating to witness a professional woman being catty with other women, or men, for that matter. According to a Workplace Bullying Institute survey, female bullies single out other females 71 percent of the time. Women enlist their peers to harass other women. Fifty-three percent of the women targeted suffered serious harm from this behavior, as opposed to 36 percent of the men who were bullied. In 2006, Madeleine Albright, former U.S. Secretary of State (and Wellesley graduate) said in her keynote speech at the "Celebrating Inspiration" luncheon with the Women's National Basketball Association's (WNBA) All-Decade Team, "There is a special place in hell for women who don't help other women." She took some heat over that comment during the 2016 Hillary Clinton presidential campaign, since many people believed she meant to support a woman no matter what the circumstance. However, what I believe she meant and what I believe personally is that women should support other women who are qualified and ready to rise higher up the career ladder.

The bullying behavior of a few women impacts the image of all women in the workplace. In contrast, if a man is a bad manager, it is just considered a personal failure and not generalized to all males' management skills. However, if a woman is a bad manager, people tend to transfer those negative traits to all women. This leads many to believe that women generally do not make good managers. In my opinion, women need to understand that what we do not only reflects upon us individually, but reflects upon women in general. I think we have to take that responsibility very seriously.

I believe that one reason women tend to find it more difficult than men in the workplace originally developed during our childhoods. When I was going through school in the 1960s and 1970s, girls' sports were not generally offered. Girls of my generation did not have the opportunity to learn what the boys learned about teamwork and goals. In the 1970s, Dr. Janet Lever of Northwestern University observed and interviewed 200 fifth graders for one year and documented how girls' and boys' activities differed. She found that 65 percent of boys' games were competitive, compared to 35 percent of girls' games. Competitive games were organized by hierarchy: coaches, team captains, star players, average players, and benchwarmers. Boys' favorite games—such as basketball, baseball, Cowboys and Indians, Cops and Robbers, football, soccer, and War—all had large numbers of participants and identified end goals to win. On the other hand, girls expressed that it was more important to be popular than to win. Their favorite games—such as hopscotch, jump rope, and tag—did not require a large number of participants and were "turn-taking" games with no expressed goal and no defined end. The skills taught in the boys' games prepared them better for future professional environments than those in the girls' games.

I discovered other differences between girls and boys at my sons' soccer games. After a game in which Matthew stole the ball from a friend on the opposing team, the two boys walked over to the sidelines together and his friend said, "Good play." One of the mothers standing next to me said, "Wow, that happened at my daughter's soccer game last month, but her friend on the other team was really upset. She said, 'I can't believe you did that to me. I thought you were my friend.'"

Luckily, girls' sports have become more prevalent in schools because of Title IX, and girls now learn more about teamwork. They are learning, just as boys do, that the goal is for their team to win. The new generation of women professionals is better equipped to focus on team success, rather than on individual accomplishments. I always try to think of the larger picture. If you help others out, they will at some future time, in turn, help you. I often notice how the expression "I owe you one" seems to be much more common with men in the workplace than with women. We women really need to think in those terms, too.

Being a woman, especially in a male-dominated field, can be like walking on a tightwire. At times, there is a fine line between a statement or an action being sexist and one being a sign of acceptance and respect. I have found that sometimes you need to lighten up and not take things so seriously. Having a sense of humor is helpful. I am in no means suggesting that women should bow down to discriminatory or misogynist statements or activities. What I am saying is that sometimes women have a preconceived notion of what is discriminatory or misogynist and lose perspective because of that notion.

Let me cite an example. When I was the director of technology for the City of Cambridge, I belonged to a professional group called the Massachusetts Government Information Systems Association. The group's members were technology directors and managers from cities and towns throughout the state. At that time, I was the only female director. There was one other municipality that had a female technology manager, but she was responsible for maintaining computer systems that were selected by upper management. I was the only female who played a strategic planning and decision-making role in technology. At first, the group's meetings were uncomfortable. I had been used to being with more women professionals when I was in Washington. Even so, I actively participated in the meetings and gained the respect of the membership. After a few years, I was asked if I would become a member of the association's board. I agreed and became the vice-president. My relationships with the other board members strengthened, and we became good friends.

One day at a board meeting held at a local restaurant, the president stood up and said he wanted to give me an award. He said, "Valerie has added diversity to our group that has always been all male. She has become one of us." He then opened a box and with a flourish proclaimed, "You are hereby awarded the Golden Jock Strap!" He had taken an actual jock strap and dyed it gold!

"You are hereby awarded the Golden Jock Strap!"

Diners at nearby tables observed what was happening and looked very uncomfortable. Most women at these other tables looked horrified. I, however, thought it was hilarious. I knew the men involved, was familiar with their sense of humor, and fully understood it was their way of accepting me into their previously old boys' network. I announced to the nearby diners, "It's okay. Really it's okay." My advice is to avoid jumping to conclusions about people's intentions without understanding the total situation and context. I do not approve of sexism, but I knew these men very well and understood what they did was humorous and out of mutual respect.

Throughout my career, each evening I asked myself whether I had acted in ways true to my character and core beliefs, no matter what pressures I was under. I realized that if I could face myself, then I could face others without reservation. Because work situations are constantly shifting, it is the character one demonstrates and the relationships one builds that are most important.

Here are some other lessons I have learned along the way.

<u>MANAGE PEOPLE WELL</u>

- Delegate. Admittedly, you know that you can do a work task faster and better, and you do not want to take the time to show others how to do it. It is most likely true, for at least the first few times, that someone else will not be as proficient. However, unless you give someone else the chance to learn, you resign yourself to the fact that you will always have to do that task. Unless you want to do it forever, you need to bite the bullet and give another person a chance to learn it.

- Be a good coach and mentor. Provide the necessary professional development and opportunities for people to learn and grow, so you can assist them along their career path. This tends to be a difficult concept for many managers. They feel threatened that their employees could take over their jobs, or that their employees might leave their company for other jobs. Although it may be risky to make colleagues aware of other opportunities, I found that employees truly appreciate it, and in turn, value working for you. There were numerous times when employees came to me to talk about a position that they became aware of and to seek my professional advice about whether it would be a good move for them before they pursued it. It was very rewarding when an employee and I could have open and honest conversations based on mutual trust and respect.

- Display confidence when you make a decision. Women typically prefer to build consensus, hearing from people with multiple perspectives and looking at as many angles as possible before making judgments. Because of this, they are skilled at finding common ground and resolving conflicts. However, sometimes this collaborative approach can be perceived by some as indecisiveness. Therefore, it is important to share the types of research or analysis you conducted and why.

- When you begin a meeting with someone in your office, close your door, set your phone to voicemail, and shut down your computer. This demonstrates that you are giving that person your full attention, and he or she will appreciate it.

- Nip performance problems in the bud. Instead of saying things like, "Your work is unacceptable," say things like, "Your work has always been of high quality and something I could depend upon. However, lately its quality has not been good, and you have made mistakes. This is just not like you. Is something going on? What do you think is causing this, and how can we fix it?"

- Do not feel guilty for saying no. When someone comes into your office to talk about something, but it is a bad time for you, it is okay to ask, "Is this an emergency, or do you think you can wait a bit? I really want to provide you with the proper attention, but right now is a tough time, and I do not think I can adequately do that." If he or she says that it can wait, immediately select another time and place to discuss it.

- Remember that an employee's performance is strongly influenced by his or her manager's behavior and the organization's climate. Do not expect employees to care about their work if they do not feel you care about them.

- If you are not sure what employees think, ask. Do not assume you know. Let them know you value their opinions, but that does not mean you will always follow their suggestions. Make sure you let them know in particular cases why you did not.

- Remove uncertainty caused by poor communication. The more that employees know about what is going on, the less they fear what they do not know about.

THE HIRING PROCESS

- How you interview, hire, and orient employees tells them a lot about your organization and sets the tone for their stay with you.

- Determine upfront which selection criteria you will use. I have always used what I call the Double A selection criteria when hiring a new employee: The two A's stand for Aptitude and Attitude. The key is to find someone who is intelligent and has a proven record to adjust and learn quickly, while also having the drive to succeed and the ability to get along with others.

- Be aware of the pace of change in your company. Information technology, the field I worked in for thirty years, used to be staffed by employees who could offer certifications in various programs and languages. Today managers like me look instead for a broad understanding of digital methods rather than specific certifications. This is because protocols and programs change, often every year. Do not hesitate to hire an employee who does not have all the certifications you need, if he or she shows proficiency in social media and research. He or she will be able to pick up the details of new programs on the job.

- Do not underestimate the importance of hiring an employee with good communication skills, an upbeat personality, willingness to help others, the drive to succeed, and the demeanor, humility, and personality to fit well into your organization.

- The goal is not only to find a person who is a good match for you, but for you to be a good match for the applicant. You do not want to invest time and effort in someone who later realizes that the job is not for them. The cost of turnover in time and team morale is just too high. Spending the additional time on the front end to find a candidate who will become a successful, long-term employee is well worth it.

- Make sure to create an inclusive hiring process. Team morale will be affected by a new hire, so the selection process should be as inclusive as possible and appropriate. My process included a series of visits and interviews with the prospective candidates. The candidates were interviewed not only by me, but also by various levels of people within the organization, similar to a 360-degree evaluation process. The candidate had group interviews with the people who would report to him or her, with the people in the department who would be his or her peers, and with anyone from other departments with whom this position worked closely.

- Explain your selection process upfront to the candidate. The candidate usually will be very appreciative (and impressed) with the care taken to try to ensure a successful long-term relationship.

- Document the decision process. I asked each person who interviewed the candidate to fill out a standard evaluation form that asked common questions, such as: "What are the candidate's strengths? What are the candidate's weaknesses? Would you bring this candidate back for a second interview? Would you hire this candidate? Do you have any additional comments you would like to share about this candidate?"

- Do comprehensive reference checking. For each candidate, if applicable, I asked for at least one reference who reported to the candidate, one who supervised the candidate, and one who was a peer of the candidate. In fairness to the candidate, I obtained two sets of references: those references who could be contacted at any time and other references who would not be contacted unless the candidate was tentatively offered the job. In addition, during my conversations with references, I tried to learn about and contact other people who knew the candidate, but were not provided as references.

- Invite the top candidate to spend a full day in the workplace. Introduce him or her to the staff to ensure the candidate is a good fit for the company. Show the candidate the range of responsibilities of the job. Let him or her experience the work environment that your company offers. Both the employee and the employer can make a better decision about working together if the workday is experienced, not just described.

<u>Communicate Effectively</u>

- Do not underestimate the power of body language, especially if you are a petite woman, like I am. At meetings, stand or sit up straight and use hand gestures, when appropriate, so that you take up as much space as possible and appear bigger. Put your hands on the table, instead of folding them in your lap or across your body. Sit closer than usual to the front edge of your chair. An upright posture affects how others see you, as well as how you see yourself. Studies have found that people who sit up straight, as opposed to slumping, have more confidence in their own ideas.

- Speak in a low voice, slowly and clearly. If you speak quickly or in a high-pitched voice, your credibility as a professional may be compromised. Breathe deeply and speak with confidence. This will help you appear calm and self-assured, even if you are not at the time.

- If a colleague co-opts your idea, speak up. Say, "I am glad you agree with me" or "You articulated my idea much better than I did. Thanks."

- In a meeting, if you are interrupted, be firm and say, "Please let me finish." If a colleague is interrupted, support her and speak up by saying something like, "Please wait a minute. I would like to hear what she was going to say."

- Speak up for what is right, especially when others are being wrongly treated. It is so frustrating to see a person—whether because of ignorance, ambition, or lack of courage—sit silently when someone is expressing untruths about others. I have learned in life that, unfortunately, when a person acts like this, others end up paying dearly for their cowardice. If it is uncomfortable or inappropriate to speak up publicly, arrange to meet with the person in private. As a professional, you are paid (and respected) for providing your honest perspectives, not for being a lap dog. As Confucius said, "To know what is right and not do it is the worst cowardice."

- Do not overuse email. If you have not resolved a situation within three rounds of email, pick up the phone or address the issue in person. There are three parts of communication—words, tone of voice, and body language. Email is the least effective form of communication because it only provides the words. A phone call is second best, as it also provides the tone of voice. The most effective form is always in person. Also, be very selective on what email you forward to others. Most people find it an annoyance to have their in-boxes cluttered with the latest joke. Let people know that when you send them an email, it is a valuable one that is worth their time to read.

- Understand your strengths and weaknesses. Studies have shown that both male and female managers perceive that women possess four types of communication skills necessary for effective management: listening, writing, verbal, and nonverbal. In addition, both male and female managers perceive four areas in which women managers need training: assertiveness, confidence building, public speaking/making presentations, and dealing with men.

- Dress for success. You want to dress in colors that flatter your skin, hair, and eye color. Color Me Beautiful (www.colormebeautiful.com) is a good resource.

- Wear the highest heels you are comfortable in, to give you some height and to benefit from the power statement they can make, especially if you are a petite ("fun-size") woman, like I am at five feet, one inch. However, you need to intelligently balance the negative health impacts of wearing high heels with their positive impacts. Some suggestions include:
  o Make sure your shoes are the right size. Your foot should not slide forward, putting even more pressure

on your toes, and the toe area should be wide enough to allow you to wiggle them.

o Wear high heels on days that require only limited walking or standing.

o Do not wear high heels all day. Take them off and wear more comfortable shoes, such as athletic or walking shoes, while driving or sitting at your desk.

o Stretch your feet and toes. Take time every day at home to stretch your calf muscles and feet. Stand on the edge of a step with your shoes off. With your weight on the balls of your feet and your heels extending off the edge, drop your heels down to stretch. You can also put a pencil on the floor and try to pick it up with your toes.

HANDLE YOUR INSECURITY

• Reach outside of yourself. Sometimes women can take comments or situations too personally and can lack confidence in providing their opinions. Taking your personal perspective out of a situation can help. Role playing can provide you with the temporary confidence of authority. For example, envision that you are an outside consultant who has been asked for input. This should help you to speak up for yourself and express your ideas.

• Be more open to taking career risks. Women tend to worry too much about whether they have the skills needed to take on a new, loftier role. When offered an opportunity, they fall back on the excuse that they are unfamiliar with that kind of work. Instead of thinking that they are not ready to do something, women need to think that they want to do it and can learn by doing it. Women need to grab for leadership roles even if they are not certain they have the credentials for that step—after all, that is what men do!

- Have one folder in your desk drawer labeled "ILM" to stand for "I Love Myself." Each and every time someone writes you a complimentary note or applauds you for something you have done, put it or a notation of it in your ILM folder—even if it is just a scrawl at the bottom of a memo. Awards or special recognitions you have received, articles or papers you have published or are cited in, and special notes from friends or family can also be placed in your ILM folder. When you are feeling stressed, take the folder out and review the contents. Do not overlook your accomplishments, wonderful qualities, and special gifts.

- Skip the people pleasing. Facebook chief executive, Mark Zuckerberg, once told Sheryl Sandberg, Facebook's chief operating officer and author of *Lean In*, that her desire to be liked by everyone would hold her back.

- Visualize your career as a jungle gym, not a ladder. This is one of my favorite tips from Sandberg's *Lean In*. A jungle gym is a great image of the 21st-century career path. "Ladders are limiting," Sandberg writes. "Jungle gyms offer more creative exploration. There are many ways to get to the top of a jungle gym. The ability to forge a unique path with occasional dips, detours and even dead ends presents a better chance for fulfillment."

<u>DIVERT DISASTERS</u>

- Lost that back of your earring right before the meeting? No problem. Cut off the tip of a pencil eraser and use that to hold your earring in place!

- Afraid of crying at an inappropriate moment? Pinch the bridge of your nose with your thumb and index finger firmly. This stimulates the oculomotor nerve that controls your eye movements. It will keep your eyes open and prevent you from tearing up. This method also works when you feel that your eyes are watering and you want to avoid making your mascara run. Also, to block your tear ducts, try putting your head back and crunching the back of your neck.

Chapter Nine
Skills For Success

When I attended Wellesley College, computer science courses were not offered and job-related internships were not common. There was no expectation of computer skills and no assumption that high school and college jobs would be career-related. The Census Bureau took a leap of faith in offering me a job, but they had confidence in my aptitude and attitude. That job kicked off my career in the field of technology, providing me with many opportunities.

Although I still believe that aptitude and attitude are critical, there is now an expectation of computer skills, although the actual skills are constantly changing. Early in my career, it was important to learn how to program in the FORTRAN computer language, and how to use the Lotus 1-2-3 software for spreadsheets. That is definitely not the case today. There

are other programming languages and spreadsheet software used in today's marketplace that employees must learn in order to succeed. Throughout time, there has always been the need to write an effective business letter, create graphs and charts of organized data, give a successful presentation, skillfully perform research, and effectively communicate. The needs may be the same, but the tools have changed. Many employers use products such as Word for word processing, Excel for charts and graphs, PowerPoint for presentations, Google search engines for research, and social media sites such as Facebook, LinkedIn, and Twitter to communicate. If you do not have the experience with the tools that the particular employer uses, then you need to prove your ability to learn new things quickly.

Professional development and continued education are keys to success. There are numerous online training sites available. Coursera, edX, Khan Academy, MIT OpenCourseWare, CreativeLive, ALISON, and Skillshare are just some of the sites currently offering both technical and nontechnical training. Consider informal ways of educating yourself through joining professional organizations, attending conferences, and keeping up with trade publications in your field. When seeking a job, look for companies that offer training programs and professional development opportunities. In job interviews, ask what kind of professional development is available.

Over the years, I have found that many skills for success have not changed a great deal. They were important 30 years ago, and I believe they will be important 30 years from now. They include the following:

BUILD YOUR NETWORK

In the 1980s, I took a one-week course on women's networking and team building. I had the opportunity to learn the skills that men had long before learned on the ballfield, in the gym, and on the golf course. I learned that the phrase, "I owe you one," was used in many male conversations, but not in any female conversations I had had. I learned the value of a win-win situation. I learned the importance of give and take, helping someone else while knowing that they would help you back. That is the key to networking, gathering allies for your career journey.

Networking is a professional necessity. If you do not build and maintain your networks properly, you will most likely lose out on opportunities, such as new information, promotions, and jobs. Whether you are an extrovert or an introvert, you can succeed in networking. It is easier for extroverts—after all, who enjoys starting a conversation with a stranger better than an extrovert? However, introverts can find success in seeking out opportunities to connect in smaller group settings or one-on-one.

Growing your network through meeting new people and belonging to professional associations is important, yet sustaining the network you already have is equally important. Some ideas for this include:

- Each month, take a person out for coffee and catch up with projects, interests, and challenges. Think of what you can do to help that person. The goal is not to ask for something, but to keep the relationship strong.

- Each week, forward a piece of information to someone who you think could benefit from it.

- Follow up with someone you connected with recently.

- Comment on social media posts, such as Facebook and LinkedIn.

- Send a thank-you note to someone who helped you.

- Compliment a person to her peers or boss.

- Introduce colleagues to other colleagues who may benefit from a relationship.

- Do a small favor for someone.

Sheryl Sandberg recommends creating what she calls a Lean-In Circle. This is a peer group of 8 to 10 women who meet monthly, offering one another encouragement and development ideas. When I worked for the City of Cambridge, although there were not many women at the top executive level, I managed to reach out and connect with other women in the organization. Through lunches, meetings, and off-hours activities, we developed friendships and relationships to support and help each other as we navigated through common challenges.

The number of all-women networking groups continues to increase, and the groups continue to benefit women seeking contacts who are experiencing similar challenges or have already succeeded in breaking through the glass ceiling. Catalyst, the nonprofit research and advisory organization that works to advance women in business and the professions, provides detailed information about creating women's internal networks. The site Quintessential Careers at www.livecareer.com/quintessential also offers advice on women's networking and professional associations.

BUILD RELATIONSHIPS

You need supportive relationships at work to succeed. And you certainly cannot achieve what you long for if you have alienated all your colleagues, peers, and managers.

Once in my career, I sadly witnessed an employee who lost sight of that importance. He was a young man who I had hired, mentored, promoted, and respected highly as a person and as a professional. He developed close relationships with the other members of the technology department and was very well respected. After 10 years in the department, he had an opportunity to transfer to a different department, a department with which he and his colleagues had had difficulties. Everyone thought it would be great for someone who had a better understanding of technology to now be an effective liaison between the two departments. However, after the transfer, he believed he could prove his loyalty to his new department members by criticizing the technology department for its policies, even many that he himself had implemented. Many members of the technology department could not believe that he would betray them that way. It was sad to see the strong personal and professional relationships destroyed that he had spent 10 years of his career cultivating. The importance of developing and nurturing relationships should never be underestimated.

A woman who I worked with at Phillips Academy sometimes called me Pollyanna, because she said I was too positive about people. She was not well-liked, but believed that because she was hardworking, she should be promoted. Sadly, she was not promoted because she was not a good team player.

A small gesture that I have found effective is to intentionally welcome a new coworker. Introduce yourself by giving one piece of friendly advice, such as the best place to grab lunch.

Sports can be a major help in building relationships. I always participated in company softball leagues, sports office pools, and other company sporting events. I never could learn to play the game of golf, but I would strongly recommend that a woman learn golf in order to participate in the company golfing tournaments.

Sports office pools are collections in which people put in a certain amount of money and place their guesses on the outcomes of sporting events. These are known as picks. The person acting as office pool manager provides a form on which these picks are written down. When the games are over, the person(s) who picked the most winners gets the money. Sports office pools come in many varieties. The most popular sports office pools involve weekly National Football League (NFL) games and the annual National Collegiate Athletic Association (NCAA) basketball tournament, known as March Madness. To learn more about this universal office activity, check out www.easyofficepools.com.

<u>FIND A MENTOR</u>

While mentoring relationships are important for everybody, they are essential for women. A mentor can protect a woman from discrimination, introduce her to the old boys' network, and help her navigate her way past career obstacles.

When I began my career, I had no idea what a mentorship was. Luckily, I fell into one. On the first day of my job at the Census Bureau, I learned that my desk furniture had yet to arrive, and I needed to sit in the office area of Bob Munsey, a branch chief in the division. We had the opportunity to get to know each other and share stories about our career paths and goals. That was the beginning of our professional relationship, mentorship, and lifelong friendship. At Phillips Academy, I learned that the business manager, Susan Stott, was a Wellesley graduate. Through lunches and meetings, we developed a mentoring relationship, and although she and I are no longer at Phillips Academy, she remains a mentor and friend.

To find a mentor, look for someone who has influence and connections within the organization, someone who you respect, and someone with whom you have something in common—such as your alma mater, mutual friends or colleagues from a previous job, or hobbies. Invite the person to lunch or to a meeting to get to know him or her better and to evaluate if your rapport is suitable for a mentoring relationship. When the time feels right, you can either directly ask the person to be your mentor, or you can say how much you value his or her experience and expertise and that you hope he or she will continue to share advice and offer you guidance.

ADVOCATE FOR YOURSELF

You have to advocate and negotiate continually—for yourself, for your staff, and for your budget. If you do not advocate for yourself, who will? I have seen that women struggle far more in this arena than men. Many women believe that if they work hard in their offices and get tasks completed, career success and promotions will naturally follow. Unfortunately, in many situations that does not happen.

It can be uncomfortable to promote yourself, especially when you are taught as a young girl to be modest and not to brag. But people inside and outside your workplace need to know about your accomplishments. You need to let others know who you are, what you have to offer, and how you make a positive impact on the organization. Here are a few ideas that I have found effective.

- Submit departmental announcements and accomplishments to the organization's internal newsletter and local publications, if appropriate.

- Send a monthly report to your boss to keep him or her updated. Include your accomplishments and accolades from the previous month, descriptions of the projects you are currently working on, and what your goals are for the upcoming month.

- Take leadership roles in professional associations and volunteer to speak at meetings.

Chapter Ten
Handling Stress

I kept a cartoon on my wall at work that showed a goldfish swimming frantically in a blender, saying, "And you thought your life was stressful." It made me laugh and helped me put things in perspective when I found myself having to deal with stress. Stress is an ever-so-popular word. "I am a bit stressed out" or "I am under a lot of stress" is a common complaint these days.

There is no doubt that too much stress is bad for you, both physically and mentally. When you are challenged, your systems go into overdrive. This is fine once or twice a day, but you do not want to get into the habit of revving up over every single challenge. Occasional stress is a plus, like a gas pedal that can propel you out of a dangerous situation fast. However, habitual stress can lead to serious health problems. Chronic stress disrupts nearly every system in your body. It can raise blood pressure, suppress your immune system, increase your risk of heart attack and stroke, contribute to infertility, and speed up your aging process. When you keep your body at high alert for years, you can even rewire your brain, leaving you more vulnerable to anxiety and depression.

When I was 29 years old, my life was difficult, verging on impossible. Tony and I had moved from Washington and were starting new jobs in Boston. We could not find a house that we could afford close to our jobs. We had a 15-month old son. My dad had been diagnosed with terminal cancer, and we were trying to deal with his illness and my mom's anguish. We lived at my parents' house, which was about a two-hour commute to and from Boston. Our days were long and arduous. We never got a break. We would wake up at 4:30 a.m. each workday, drop Matthew off at the house of a family friend who had agreed to take care of him, drive together more than two hours to our jobs, work until 5 p.m., drive to the Lahey Clinic in Burlington, Massachusetts, to spend time with my dad, then pick up Matthew, and finally arrive back at my parents' house at about 8 p.m. We would spend a little time with Matthew before putting him to bed, spend some time with my mom, collapse into our own bed around 11:30 p.m., and start all over the next day. On weekends, we would visit my dad and meet with real estate agents to try to find housing closer to work.

That was our life. It was not what we had hoped for when we moved back to New England. I dreamed of the day when we could establish a better routine. Five months later, my dad died, and for the next three months we helped my mom transition to widowhood and then we finally found a house. I learned that stressful situations continue. They truly never go away; they just change.

Years later, when my boys were 10 and 6 years old, I came home from work one evening and began to vent to my husband about the stressful things that happened to me at the office. That might have included an annoying thing a coworker said or did, a bothersome new policy, or a computer crashing. My sons looked up at me and one of them asked, "Mommy, why are you upset?" When I tried to explain, I noticed the bewilderment in my boys' eyes as they tried hard to understand. That was when I realized how ridiculous it was to waste time on such minor problems. Throughout the years since then, when I have had moments of stress, I have pictured myself trying to explain the situation to my two young boys, and that has helped me put things into the proper perspective.

I also eventually realized that there is a point of diminishing returns. I was working harder and harder, but not getting as much done. This makes me think of the tale of the old woodcutter who was feverishly trying to cut down a tree with his ax, sweat pouring from his face. A man walking by said, "Hey, you should stop and sharpen that ax." However, the woodcutter just gasped and replied, "Can't. Too busy." It is so hard to grasp the concept that we all need to take some time out to rethink our strategy and replenish our energy. Make sure to take that break for lunch or go for a quick walk, so you can return to your project with better direction and renewed drive.

Here are some additional strategies to manage stress.

Keep Difficulties in Perspective

- Draw a circle to represent the pie of your life. Decide on which six to eight major parts of your life are most important to you and draw in the lines to represent what size slices you want to give them. For example, my six pieces are: Family, Friends, Career, Personal Health, Personal Growth and Development, and Community Service. Keep this circle in your desk drawer, so that you can remind yourself of your priorities and the many facets of your life. When you find yourself feeling stressed about one aspect of your life, such as work, look at your Life Pie. It will help you to maintain your balance and avoid thinking that everything in your life is going wrong. Also, in everyone's life, there are people who get in your way and stress you out. For example, at work there may be someone who is making it difficult for you to do your job. Represent such a person with a small dot in the Career piece of your pie.

131

A dot in the Community Service piece of the pie might be a neighbor who is undermining you at zoning meetings. Now look at the entire pie, see the small dots in just two pieces of it, and realize how irrelevant those people really are. They do not merit that much attention in your life. However, if you see more than four dots in a piece of the pie, you may want to rethink the way you are doing things or see if there is someone who can assist you.

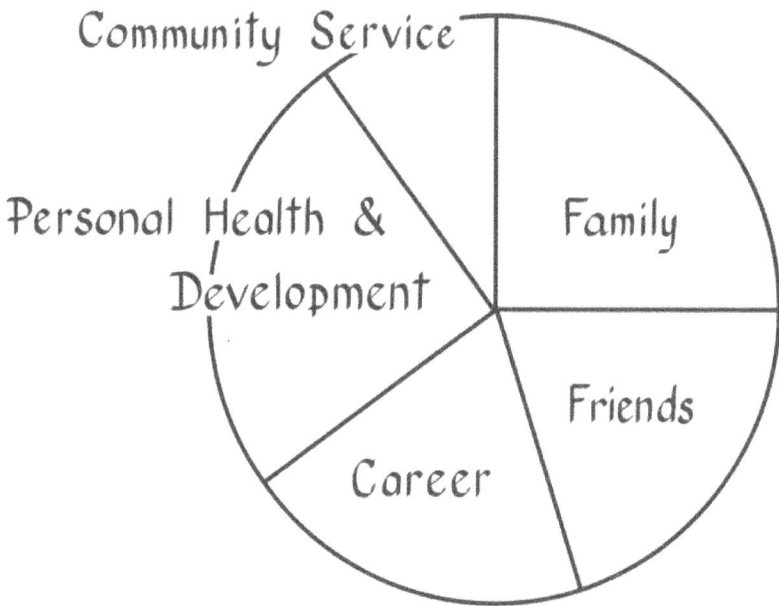

- Give yourself a wake-up call to keep things in perspective. This may sound morbid, but when you are stressed and think you have problems, imagine that your child or someone else very close to you has just been injured in an automobile accident. You would pour all of your energy into that crisis, and all your other problems would immediately become irrelevant. In this way, you imagine how bad your situation could be, in order to jolt yourself into appreciating your life as it is.

- Every time you feel yourself getting pulled into other people's nonsense, remember the old Polish proverb: "Not my circus, not my monkeys."

- Being angry with someone or holding a grudge is like you taking poison and expecting the other person to die. Forgive people, not because they deserve forgiveness, but because you deserve peace. None of us can eliminate anger completely from our lives, but remember that carrying it with us can be bad for our health.

- For each important decision that you need to make, ask yourself these questions: "What is the worst thing that could happen, and could I live with that? What is the best thing that could happen, and am I willing to take the risk in order to have that chance?"

- Research shows that in those areas in which we have experience and expertise, our unconscious minds are equipped to make the best choice in a situation, based on the information available. And that the quicker you make that choice, the more likely you are to make the right one. Going with your first instinct is often the right way to go. Develop intuition and trust it.

BREATHE DEEPLY AND MEDITATE

- Learn how to breathe deeply. Deep breathing releases toxins and tension from your body. The key to deep breathing is to inhale so completely that the air fills your lungs all the way down into your belly. Put your hand on your abdomen so that you can feel it expand. Dr. Andrew Weil on his YouTube channel recommends this 4-7-8 breathing exercise: Exhale completely through your mouth, making a whooshing sound; close your mouth and inhale quietly through your nose to a count of four; hold your breath for a count of seven; then exhale completely through your mouth, making a whooshing sound to a count of eight. Repeat this cycle three more times.

- Pause. Whether you call it meditation, silence, or prayer, pausing in this way for just a few minutes a day can help you recharge your batteries and make you feel happier.

- Instead of going skiing or sailing on vacation, take a trip to a spiritual destination. When I visited Tibet, I saw how its people seemed so peaceful and relaxed. I now have made a simple Tibetan meditation technique part of my normal day. Several times each day, I stop whatever I am doing or thinking and just am. I become aware of my breathing and experience the moment. Many spiritual centers sponsor weekend retreats where you can learn and practice techniques like this one.

- Practice meditation. Select a meditation mantra, a word that you will repeat during your meditation to help you focus. You can use a common word, such as "relax," or one from numerous traditional meditation mantras on the Internet. The one I use is "Om." Once you have your mantra, you will be ready to start a meditation tradition in your life. Sit comfortably in a quiet room and gently close your eyes. Take a deep breath through your nose. As you exhale, say your mantra quietly. Continue deep breathing and saying your mantra for two minutes. Try to build up to 20 minutes each day.

- Practice progressive muscle relaxation (PMR). Breathe deeply, while you purposely tense and then release separate muscle groups. Begin at your feet. Tense your toes for a count of eight and then release. Then tighten the muscles in your legs for a count of eight and release. Next, your stomach muscles, then your hands, arms, neck, and face. This takes a total of only five minutes and can be done at your desk or even in your car in a parking lot.

<u>RELIEVE YOUR "LIFE CAN BE A PAIN IN THE NECK" PROBLEM</u>

- To ease a tense neck, fill a large resealable plastic bag with three to four cups of foam packing peanuts. Leaving some air in the bag, seal it tightly, put it into a pillowcase, and position it behind your head in a bubble bath. The air in the pillow cushions your head and neck and the packing peanuts gently massage your sore spots.

- Rub your earlobes between your thumbs and forefingers. Massaging these acupressure points can clear your head and dull any pain there and in your neck.

- For neck and shoulder stretches that feel good, bend your head as if trying to touch your right ear to your right shoulder and hold for 10 seconds. Do the same on your left side. Then try to touch your chin to your chest and hold. Lift your shoulders tightly toward your ears, hold, and then very slowly bring them back down. Repeat each of these movements at least four times. This exercise can be done sitting down at a desk or in an easy chair.

<u>CREATE WAYS TO RELAX</u>

- Take a picture or buy a postcard of a beautiful scene when you are on vacation. Tack it on your bulletin board at work. When in need of quick stress relief, stare at the picture or postcard and imagine you are there again.

- Buy a Christmas ornament whenever you travel. During the holidays, if you feel a bit stressed, these ornaments on your tree will remind you of happy times.

- Keep pink-colored things near you or within reach. The electromagnetic frequency of the color pink can prompt your brain to release serotonin, a neurotransmitter that helps you feel better.

- Have fun with a coloring book. Coloring is a hobby that we typically think only toddlers and kindergarteners could enjoy, but it turns out that even adults can benefit from it. Many psychologists recommend coloring, because it helps relieve tension by unlocking our memories of childhood and simpler times. Psychologist Carl Jung used to have his patients color as a way of getting them to focus and to allow their subconscious to let go.

- Visit or call a friend, coworker, relative, or neighbor. Studies have found that people who are alone or who avoid public interaction feel more stressed and tired compared to their more sociable counterparts. People who see their friends frequently are among the healthiest psychologically, as activities that provide social support help relieve their stress and build their emotional energy.

- Laugh! Watch a funny television show or movie, read a joke book, watch a humorous video on YouTube, or just go into a room and laugh out loud.

- Keep a journal. Each evening at the end of a stressful day, take 10 minutes to write down your feelings. Keeping a journal can help you let go of negative thoughts that nag you, freeing your brain to deal with each new day.

- Try to go to bed by 10 p.m. According to Ayurveda, the ancient medical tradition of India, one hour of sleep before midnight is worth two hours of sleep after midnight. "Beauty sleep" is traditionally sleep enjoyed before midnight. Try going to bed before 10 p.m. for three nights in a row and feel the difference.

ENERGIZE AND CALM YOURSELF WITH FOODS AND SCENTS

- Sprinkle powdered ginger on foods, such as carrots or sweet potatoes, or have ginger candy on hand. Ginger boosts your mood by helping to stabilize your blood sugar levels.

- Drink a cup of green tea. It also contains theanine, which has a stress-reducing effect on your brain, so it can calm you while giving you mental clarity.

- Eat one ounce of dark chocolate per day. A single serving can rid you of the blues in as few as 10 minutes.

- Take two grams of fish oil daily. Research at Harvard Medical School shows that it can increase your physical and mental energy by 63 percent and boost your mood by 50 percent or more.

- Pop a peppermint. The smell of peppermint can lower fatigue, increase alertness, and decrease frustration.

- Try aromatherapy using essential oils. The oils can be used directly from the bottle (you can dab lemon oil, for example, under your nose), in lotions that contain the oils, or in room mists that contain the oils. However, be careful if you suffer from asthma or allergies. The National Association of Holistic Aromatherapy (www.naha.org) suggests using the essential oils in the table at the top of the next page to relieve the accompanying symptoms.

- Research posted on www.aromaweb.com indicates that certain essential oils can also improve certain emotions. Refer to the table at the bottom of the next page.

ESSENTIAL OILS AND THEIR PRIMARY USES

Chamomile	Helps to relieve sleeplessness, anxiety, headaches, muscle aches, and tension. Also useful in treating wounds and infection.
Eucalyptus	Helps to treat respiratory problems, such as coughs, colds, and asthma. Also useful in boosting the immune system and relieving muscle tension.
Lavender	Helps to relieve sleeplessness, headaches, and migraines. Helps to balance hormones in women, balance skin, and soothe minor cuts and burns when used as an antiseptic. Can be both relaxing and uplifting, helping to treat depression.
Lemon	Helps to relieve depression, lessen stress, enhance one's mood, and relax.
Peppermint	Helps to treat headaches, muscle aches, fatigue, and digestive disorders, such as indigestion.
Rosemary	Helps to stimulate mentally, as well as to stimulate the immune and digestive systems. Good for muscle aches and tension. Can be uplifting.
Sage	Helps to treat muscular aches and pains, digestive problems, and mental disorders, such as Alzheimer's and depression.

EMOTIONS IMPROVED THROUGH USE OF KEY ESSENTIAL OILS

Anger	Chamomile, Jasmine, Orange, Rose
Anxiety, Stress, and Depression	Chamomile, Frankincense, Geranium, Grapefruit, Jasmine, Lavender, Mandarin, Rose, Sage, Sandalwood
Lack of Confidence	Cypress, Grapefruit, Jasmine, Orange, Rosemary
Fatigue, Exhaustion, and Burnout	Basil, Black Pepper, Cypress, Frankincense, Ginger, Grapefruit, Jasmine, Lemon, Peppermint, Rosemary, Sage
Fear	Chamomile, Frankincense, Grapefruit, Jasmine, Lemon, Orange, Sage
Lack of Happiness and Peace	Frankincense, Geranium, Grapefruit, Lemon, Orange, Rose, Sandalwood
Poor Memory and Concentration	Basil, Black Pepper, Cypress, Lemon, Peppermint, Rosemary, Sage

Realize and accept that stress does exist, and you are not expected to handle each trying time with perfect ease. There are things that happen in our lives that are bad, and we have to give ourselves some leeway to deal with them. Dr. Thomas H. Holmes and Richard H. Rahe of the University of Washington drew up a scale of stressful life events that appear to make people more susceptible to illness. The Holmes-Rahe Scale assigns values to these events, and the higher the score, the more stressful and potentially harmful the event. Acknowledge that these types of events do cause stress and that you may want to seek help to cope with them. The Holmes-Rahe Scale of impact per event includes the following:

THE HOLMES-RAHE STRESS INVENTORY

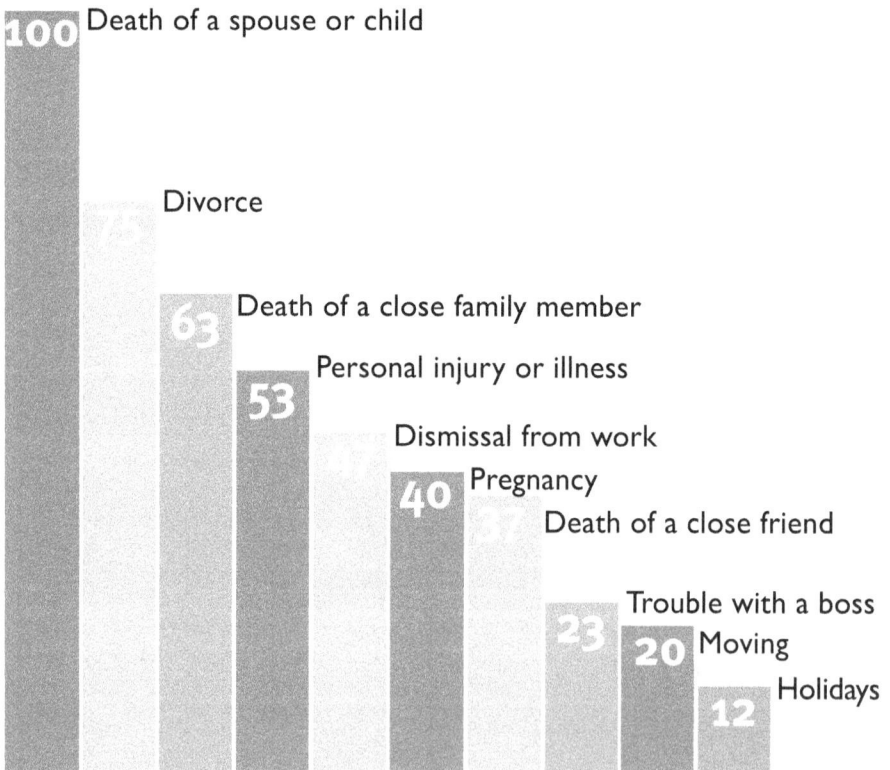

100 Death of a spouse or child

Divorce

63 Death of a close family member

53 Personal injury or illness

Dismissal from work

40 Pregnancy

Death of a close friend

Trouble with a boss

23

20 Moving

12 Holidays

Chapter Eleven
Saving Time

Everyone has 24 hours each day, so why do some people think they just do not have enough time, while others seem fine with the time they have? I have come to realize that you just need to think of ways to make the best use of those hours.

Put yourself on a time budget. First of all, eight hours should be dedicated to sleep. Then one hour can be taken for showering, dressing, checking your messages, and eating a good breakfast. So that leaves 15 hours. If you work full time (eight hours, plus a one-hour lunch), have a half-hour commute, and spend an hour for dinner, that uses up another 11 hours. So you are down to four hours to spend as you please. Your goal is to spend some of that time with your children, some with your spouse, some on routine chores, and some on your own personal and social welfare needs, such as exercising, talking or visiting with friends, reading, or going to a spa for a massage. Thinking of my day in time blocks helped me realize that I had control over that certain block of time. I could go to an exercise class, get a manicure, have dinner with my husband, or play cards with my mother in the four hours that I had free each weekday. I was often able to combine socializing with my favorite activities, such as playing tennis with my husband or going for a walk with my children. There is enough time in the day to enjoy life as well as to earn a living, if you plan carefully.

For more than a decade, Tony worked in Boston and I worked in Cambridge, so we commuted together. Near the end of the drive, I would drop off Tony at the subway near his office and continue on to my workplace. After work, we would coordinate to meet at the subway station and commute home together. Our commute time provided a wonderful opportunity for us to talk, solve problems, share information, and make plans. We did have to learn the limits for which topics we could discuss in the car, though: After all, if we got into an argument, there was no place to escape! If you do have the opportunity to share your commute with someone in your life, it really can be a time saver, as well as a gas saver.

Similarly, when my son, Matthew, was a toddler, his day care was in Somerville, Massachusetts, near to where I worked, so he commuted with my husband and me. When Matthew was not sleeping, we would sing songs and play games with him. Most of the games were educational in nature. We would sing the alphabet, quiz each other on the spelling of words, and ask simple addition or subtraction questions. Matthew had fun, and Tony and I were happy to put the time to good use.

Later in my career when I commuted alone, I would listen to the radio to get up-to-date news (and sports) and listen to tapes to learn a new language or new management skills.

MAKE THE BEST USE OF YOUR TIME

- Live by the two-minute rule: If a task can be done in less than two minutes, do it now.

- Live by the 80–20 rule, otherwise known as the Pareto Principle. Look at everything in your life based on these two questions: Which 20 percent of sources are causing 80 percent of your problems and unhappiness? Which 20 percent of sources are resulting in 80 percent of your desired outcomes and happiness? Try to change (or avoid) the unhappiness generators and increase your time with the happiness generators.

- Is someone staying too long in your office? Stand up, and while you are talking to him or her, walk to the door, open it, and say, "Thank you for coming to see me" or "This was helpful. We can follow up on this topic soon." Then stop talking. If the person persists, you are entitled to say, "I do not have any more time to talk now. We can talk again soon." Look directly at the person and say good-bye, firmly and pleasantly.

- When scheduling a meeting, send out the agenda for comments in advance. Start the meeting with, "What do we want the outcome of this meeting to be?" Invite adjustments to the agenda and end discussion points with, "What are the next steps? Who is responsible for them?" Keep posing simple questions to keep the meeting moving along.

- Write things down, so you will not waste time trying to remember them. You will have your ideas and appointments safely saved, instead of having lost them somewhere in the depths of your mind.

- Although promised the paperless office years ago, you will most likely still receive memos, trade journals and magazines, forms to fill out, and copies of articles through interoffice mail. To keep up with the inevitable paper materials, create a reading folder. When waiting for a meeting to start or a doctor's appointment, read from it. Not only are you informing yourself, but you are not stressed about having to wait.

- Open mail while standing by the recycling bin to save time discarding the junk. To cut down on junk mail, visit the Direct Marketing Association's website, at www.dmachoice.org, and ask to be removed from unwanted direct-mail lists.

- To reduce telephone tag, always suggest in your voicemail message a good time for the person to return your call.

- Do one thing at a time and finish it. If you are not able to complete it, set an interim goal for yourself (such as "complete draft" or "set up draft agenda") and stick with that one step until you finish it. Your brain must refocus each time it switches activities, and the more complicated the task, the more time it takes to refocus. The time lost can be as little as a tenth of a second or as long as 20 minutes per switch. That adds up over the course of a day.

- Delegate lower priority tasks to other people.

T<small>AKE</small> A<small>DVANTAGE OF</small> N<small>EW</small> T<small>ECHNOLOGIES</small>

- Get an EZ-Pass electronic tag for your car, if you use toll roads and bridges. It is not only faster, but you save money because the tolls are discounted.

- Invest in a smartphone to have access not only to phone calls, but also to email and the Internet. Keep in touch with friends during unexpected downtime.

- Use an electronic calendar. It is great for setting up and automatically alerting you to recurring events and appointments, such as birthdays, committee meetings, and classes.

- Pay your bills online through your bank's website. You save the time you would have spent writing out checks and envelopes, finding and attaching stamps, and going to the mailbox.

- Make use of digital video recording technology, such as DVRs and TIVOs. An average 60-minute television show has about 20 minutes' worth of commercial interruptions. You can watch your favorite show in 33 percent less time by bypassing those commercials.

- Screen phone calls through caller ID or an answering machine. If you see a phone number that you do not recognize, or it comes up as "Restricted" or "Caller Unknown", let it go to voicemail. In many cases, they are telemarketers and will not leave a message. Unless you are expecting an important call from someone, let the calls go to voicemail and check them all later in the day.

- Use Really Simple Syndication (RSS), a technology that allows you to receive up-to-date information from websites in one spot, where you can then read them on your own time. There are numerous ways to set this up. One way is to open a free account with a news aggregator, such as Feedly. Feedly (www.feedly.com) is an application that works with numerous web browsers and mobile devices, and is also available as a cloud-based service. It gathers news feeds from a variety of online sources. You can have it gather stories from your favorite news outlets, e.g. the *New York Times*, or on a topic of interest, such as climate change.

- Maximize your time on the computer by improving your typing. Sites such as www.typingmaster.com can help. When I was in high school in the early 1970s, I was mad that the girls had to take typing classes while the boys could take shop classes, which seemed like so much more fun. But now I realize that my fast typing skills have really paid off, while the boys' one-shelf handmade bookcases are probably stored in their basements.

- Back up your data to a flash drive or to a free online service, such as Google Drive or Microsoft's OneDrive. How much time would you lose if your hard drive crashed? Data loss statistics reveal that more than 22 percent of computer users say backing up information is on their to-do list, but they seldom do it. Nine percent admit they have never backed up their files.

- Learn keyboard shortcuts instead of using the mouse for your common software applications. A reference site for shortcuts for various software applications can be found at www.keyboardshortcuts.org. For example, in Microsoft Word, the entire list of keyboard shortcuts can be found by clicking on the Help tab at the very top of your screen.

COMMON PC KEYBOARD SHORTCUTS

What You Are Trying To Do	Shortcut
Copy a section of text you have highlighted	Hold down your keyboard Ctrl and then C keys simultaneously (Ctrl+C)
Save a document	Ctrl+S
Paste text	Ctrl+V
Delete text	Ctrl+X
Redo the last action	Ctrl+Y
Undo the last action	Ctrl+Z
Move to the beginning of the document	Ctrl+Home
Move to the end of the document	Ctrl+End

SIMPLIFY, SIMPLIFY, SIMPLIFY

- Consider giving cash or gift cards for presents. I used to feel guilty about it, thinking that it was too impersonal. Then I realized that I, myself, would rather receive a gift card to a favorite restaurant, movie theater, store, or spa, instead of another necklace or sweater. The key is to make it personal. Cash is often appreciated by young people in debt, so include a note that says how you hope the extra money will help. Give a cinema gift card to your sister and her family who enjoy going to the movies, a spa gift card to a friend who has had a stressful time, or a restaurant gift card for your friend's favorite eatery.

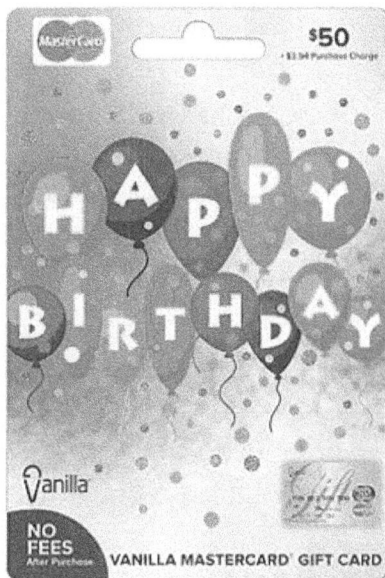

- Simplify your space. For example, only keep two pens on your desk. You will spend less time searching and choosing among numerous writing instruments. If you feel the need to have extra writing implements, put them in a drawer or a closed box, so they are there for special needs.

SCHEDULE YOUR TIME EFFECTIVELY

- Keep interruptions at a minimum. Set regular times, such as once every two hours, or an hour in the morning and an hour in the afternoon, to go through your email or voicemail, rather than responding as each message comes in.

- Plan ahead. Keep a running list of things you need to purchase. Consolidate travel to accomplish your errands, instead of driving back and forth every time you need something. As I think of errands I need to run, I add them to a list and then plan out how many trips (I hope not more than one or two) I will need to complete them.

- When making an appointment, try to get in early. The later in the day you book a doctor's visit, a haircut, or a meeting, the greater the chance it will be delayed.

TIPS TO LIVE BY

- Occasionally stop and set aside time to take inventory of your life. Ask yourself if you are spending your time on what is important to you and if you are doing what it takes to improve your life.

- Learn to say no. If you say yes to every request, you will never have any free time. Imagine saying no to each request you receive. Stick to no unless there is a good reason to say yes. Think of yes as the exception, not the rule.

• As the theme of this book conveys, realize that perfection is an illusion. We strive for perfection, because we have an image in our minds of what we should be. Realize that perfection and imperfection are defined in our own minds; they do not exist in reality. Do not let perfectionism paralyze you.

• Keep a list of your mistakes and the consequences of them. You will be surprised that many of the things you did wrong eventually turn out right. People have to make mistakes in order to grow. Mistakes do not waste time if you learn from them; they are feedback, not failure. Remember, doing okay is usually okay. Save doing great for the important stuff.

Chapter Twelve
Organizing the Office

I first learned about organizational techniques from my father. During my childhood, the General Electric plant where he worked would close down for two weeks each summer. Dad spent the first week preparing for our annual camping trip to the White Mountains. Dad would take out his worn, yellowing stenographer's notebook that listed everything that needed to be packed and where it would be located in the family station wagon. It made me smile to see him take such pleasure in checking an item off the list or giving me or my mother the next assignment. "Aye, aye, Sir," I would say, as I saluted him for his efficiency and organization. He would smile back and say, "It pays to be prepared." I guess those trips planted the seed of my extreme desire for organization.

Here are some tactics I have found helpful to keep me more organized.

- Use a tickler filing system. This tool has been my organizational savior for storing the numerous types of paper items I receive, such as notices or tickets for upcoming events, documents for meetings, and other items that I want to be reminded of by date.

This is how to set up your tickler filing system:

o   Take 44 manila folders.

o   Label 31 of the folders with the numerals 1 through 31 to represent each day of the month.

o   Label an additional 12 folders with the headings January through December for each month of the year.

o   Label the last folder as Next Year.

o   In your desk's file drawer, place the January folder first; next the 1 through 31 folders; next the February through December folders; and lastly the Next Year folder.

o   When January 1 is over, move the 1 folder behind the February folder.

o   When January is over, place the January folder after the December folder.

o   In each number-dated folder, put the paper materials you will need for whatever you have planned. Put in tickets for events on the day that they occur. Add reminder notes for special occasions and birthdays ahead of the dates. Let us say you get tickets for a Red Sox game on June 6. Put them in the June folder when they arrive. When May 6 passes and you move the 6 folder after the June folder, put the tickets into it.

o   At the end of each day, look at the folder for the day ahead. Every Friday, look at the folders for the week ahead.

•   Set up a folder organizer on your desk with four folders labeled as Calls, Paperwork, Waiting For, and Reading. When you receive a message to call someone, file it in the Calls folder. When you receive paperwork that needs to be processed, file it in the Paperwork folder. If you have placed an order for something, file it in your Waiting For folder. If you receive something that will take time to read, slip it into your Reading folder. Toward the end of each day, open these folders and do what needs to be done all at once.

- Find an organization method or program that works for you. I found David Allen's *Getting Things Done* to be very helpful in keeping me organized and in control. It is not only a book; it is also available as seminars, webinars, and CDs. More information can be found at www.davidallengtd.com

- Use the word "Unsubscribe" as a filter to send marketing email to a separate folder or directly to trash.

CLICK HERE to Unsubscribe

- Consider using services, such as Unroll.Me (https://unroll.me) to organize or easily unsubscribe from email subscriptions.

- Sort through your email daily. Keeping your in-box full is like taking all of the papers in your office and putting them on your desk. Here is a filing system that can help.
  1. Create an Action email folder.
  2. Create a Finished email folder with subfolders by subject.
  3. When you receive an email, decide if there is some action that you need to take or some task that needs to be completed as a result of the email.
  4. If it generates a project or a specific task that has a deadline, and if you have an electronic task list as part

of your system, type in the name of the project or task and drag the email to the task list. If you do not have an electronic task list, make one in a word processing document or create a master task list on paper.

5. If you will need to reply to the email, immediately hit Reply and save the blank response to your Drafts folder. Then set aside time each day to work through the drafts.

6. Decide what to do with the original email. Move it to the Action folder or move it to the subfolder in the Finished folder that represents its subject or topic, to store for later reference. You can also print and delete it, or simply delete it.

7. Once the task is completed, remember to delete the email from the Action folder, or move it to the relevant subfolder in the Finished folder.

• Process less important tasks by batch. There are many little tasks you need to do throughout the day, and you want to avoid having them interrupt more important things. To be more productive, batch them and do them all at once, preferably toward the end of the day.

• Create a consistent system for digital filing so that you always know where - or how - to find computer documents. For example, I have a folder named Academic Committee on Technology that holds all the files related to that committee. I use the same format for the date and the same naming format for each file: yyyy-mm-dd-Type. Hence, meeting minutes would be named yyyy-mm-dd-Minutes. Use key words when naming folders and files. This will make it much easier to find an item, whether you are looking through a folder, or have to input key words into your computer's search function.

- Get into the habit of writing your to-do list using just one tool, such as a pad of paper or a stenographer's notebook, a Day-Timer planner, Microsoft Outlook, or Google Tasks.

- Take time at the end of each workday or evening to plan the next 24 hours. Write up a to-do list with your have-to's and your want-to's for the next day. You will be surprised at how planning for the day increases your efficiency.

- If you use a paper calendar, transfer all recurring due dates and events (such as birthdays, anniversaries, and tax payments) to your new calendar, right before a new year begins.

GOAL THREE
RAISE A HAPPY FAMILY

Goal Three
Raise a Happy Family

Six months after my arrival in Washington, D.C., I met Tony, who worked down the hall from me at the Census Bureau. He grew up in a small town in Pennsylvania, earned his bachelor's and master's degrees from Penn State, and was a mathematical statistician. His calm demeanor was a great balance for my excitable personality. Both of us had grown up in small towns and shared similar goals and values on family and life.

Four years later, Tony and I got married and had the big Greek wedding of which my parents had always dreamed. My dad was so pleased to participate in the planning process and was so organized that, in the basement, he developed the reception seating arrangement by setting up a flip chart on graph paper with cutouts of tables and chairs sized to proportion, with a guest's name written on each chair. The event brought out over 200 people. My wedding party was huge, and Pam was my matron of honor. My mother looked beautiful in her special-order gown. My dad walked me down the aisle, cried during our father-daughter dance, and treated everyone to drinks all night. I can still remember the happiness on Mom's and Dad's faces.

After the reception, they invited everyone to their house to continue the celebration. There they took me aside and said, "This is the best day of our lives. We are so happy and so proud of you."

Wow, I had graduated from college, I had a career, and I had had the big Greek wedding! I had succeeded. Unfortunately, it came at a price, as Pam was now resentful of me for accomplishing it all and angry at my parents for being so proud of me.

As the years went by, Donna Reed became a topic of humor between my mother and me. How we giggled as we watched *It's a Wonderful Life* or repeats of *The Donna Reed Show*, saying "God, don't you just hate that woman?" I would joke and say, "Mom, if I have a girl, I will name her after you—Donna." She was able to laugh about it, and we would tease each other. Ironically, I learned later that Donna Reed was quite different from her television persona. She was a feminist, insisting on earning a college degree before she launched her acting career, protesting the Vietnam War, and suing the production company of the television show *Dallas* for breach of contract after she was abruptly fired. How flimsy the perfect housewife fantasy was!

After three years of marriage, Tony and I took jobs in the Boston area and moved with Matthew to be closer to my family. Within three months, my dad was diagnosed with terminal cancer and died two months later. My dreams of all of us being together again were destroyed. I had wanted my children to grow up with my parents and my sister's family; instead, my son witnessed the emotional devastation that his grandfather's death had on us. Without my father, my sister's relationship with my mother and the rest of us became more strained, and she skipped many holidays with us. But my mother and I grew even closer. Tony and I purchased a house in Windham, New Hampshire, about 50 miles from Somersworth, so we could visit and create memories with her.

When my second son, David, was born two years later, my mom was able to help. Although I was still sad that my dad was not alive, at least the dream of my kids spending time with my mom could become reality. Then, a few months later, my mother was diagnosed with colon cancer, the same cancer that had taken my father. We sought medical help from Dr. Herbert Hoover at Massachusetts General Hospital, renowned for his work with colon cancer (and grandson of President Herbert Hoover). He promised me that the fear I had of my father's story repeating itself would not come to pass. However, two years later, my mom's cancer returned.

After an experimental procedure was attempted, we were told that her case was now terminal. So we made the most of our time together, talking a lot about our hopes and dreams. I will always remember her saying to me one

At the age of 34, I became an orphan.

month before she died, "Val, when I do leave this earth, I want you to know that you have absolutely nothing to regret. You have always been a loving daughter and have always been there for me. You have tickled my heart, and most of all, you never expected me to be Donna Reed."

And then on April 25, 1991, she left me. At the age of 34, I became an orphan.

My mother, who met all of my ideals of a wonderful mother, lived her life with a feeling of failure. Here was a woman who fulfilled everything that Donna Reed represented, sacrificing her own desires and needs, yet still felt that she could not meet those expectations of being the "perfect woman." If she could not meet those expectations, I knew that I absolutely had no shot at meeting them! I realized the futility and harmful consequences of striving for perfection and living your life trying to be like someone else.

Hillary Clinton once said she owed her inspiration to her mother. Like my mother, Clinton's mother also had a very difficult childhood and never got a chance to go to college, but instilled in her daughter a belief that she could become whatever she wanted to become. I feel exactly the same way as Clinton. I wanted to be the wonderful mother that my mother was, plus the career woman that she never was but wanted me to be.

The transition from a single woman to a wife can be difficult for some women. You now need to take another person into consideration when making decisions and now need to share your physical space. Fortunately, Tony and I lived together before we married. I know that living together before marriage is much more commonplace in this 21st century, but some people still do not believe in it, even numerous older members of my own family. However, it really made our transition much easier. We became well aware of each other's habits, especially the quirky and annoying ones, and learned the meaning of sharing and compromising. I would not be disheartened to hear loud snoring on our wedding night, and Tony would not be shocked to find out that I was not Donna Reed. He knew upfront that I did not plan to provide home-cooked meals regularly, did not plan to keep the house meticulously spotless, and certainly did not plan to wear dresses, heels, and pearls while relaxing at home. Living together first was the right decision for us.

The biggest change for me when I got married was getting used to my new name. I was now Valerie Roman, instead of Valerie Anthonakes. It was a great change. I had often joked with friends that I would only date men with last names of six letters or fewer that were easy to pronounce—and I married one!

Another interesting shift that occurred for me after getting married was that I became even more fiscally responsible. Frugality was something that I was taught from childhood and was part of my family's DNA. I do not want to sound like the father in *My Big Fat Greek Wedding*, but it is true that the word "economy" derives from the Greek language. Originally the Greek word *oikonomou* was defined as somebody who was responsible for all the resources in a home or on an estate.

Since the proper stewardship of resources used the least amount of them, "economy" took on the meaning of frugality.

Now that I was married, I had even more reasons to make sure that our resources were managed well. After all, Tony and I were responsible for making sure our future children could grow up in a safe neighborhood with a high quality school system and could go to college. My sense of fiscal responsibility has served my family well, but the downside has been my difficulty to accept others' generosity. Instead of appreciating a generous gift or gesture and just saying "Thank you so much," my tendency has been to respond with "You shouldn't have." One of my dearest friends was very annoyed with that response, believing that I was taking the fun out of gift giving. I have since learned to look at a gift from others as allowing them to experience the joyous feeling of giving, as I always do.

If you think the transition from being a single woman to being a wife is tough, get ready for the transition from wife to mother. I was frequently told that once you become a mother, nothing will ever be the same, and you cannot go back. That is absolutely true. If you make a mistake getting married, you can get divorced, as about half of married couples do. But once you become a mother, you will always be a mother. There are no escape hatches. Before I got pregnant, Tony and I really thought long and hard to make sure we were ready for that commitment.

My journey into motherhood was not a typical one. A few years before getting married, I had hyperthyroidism, which was due to an overactive thyroid gland. It was a condition with some great features: I had so much energy plus I could eat and eat and eat—and lose weight!—at the same time. Tony frequently reminds me of how I could out-eat him with ease. When we went out for dinner, I would have a huge meal and finish it off with a hot fudge sundae. Then 30 minutes after arriving home, I would be hungry and make myself two peanut butter and jelly sandwiches. If it were not for the heart palpitations and headaches, and the fact that my weight fell to 90 pounds, I probably would not have gone to a doctor to treat my condition.

But I did and was given radioactive iodine to deactivate some of my thyroid gland. I was warned that the only risk was that within 10 to 20 years, my thyroid function could reduce to a point at which I could develop *hypo*thyroidism, an *under*active thyroid. If and when that happened, I would need to take medication for the rest of my life. Unfortunately, I was given too much of the radioactive iodine, and hypothyroidism developed after just one year. But then the doctor informed me that because of the amount of radioactive iodine I received, I might never be able to have children. I was devastated.

After Tony and I had been married for a year, we decided that we would try to have a baby. I knew it was going to be difficult, so I took out just about every book in the library about infertility. I bought the basal thermometer and made a year's worth of copies of the graph that I planned to fill out each month to track my ovulation cycle and body temperature. I did everything the way I was supposed to, and at the end of the first month, I reviewed my graph and noticed that it looked just like it should. Could I be pregnant on our first try? Yes, indeed! I decided that if we had a boy, we would name him Matthew, which means "Gift from God."

My pregnancy with Matthew continued to make my motherhood journey adventurous. Our first step was to find an obstetrician, and a close friend of ours recommended an obstetrical practice in Arlington, Virginia. As Tony and I sat in the waiting room, we noticed one of the physicians in the practice was listed as Dr. Beaver. We giggled, thinking that was a funny name for a gynecologist/obstetrician. I whispered in Tony's ear, "I wonder what his first name is." Tony jokingly responded, "I hope it's not Harry." Wouldn't you know it, his name was Dr. Harry Beaver, and he was assigned to be our obstetrician!

During my fifth month, I became ill and spent a day in bed with a fever that rose to 102.5 degrees. I called my mother to tell her how lousy I felt, and she asked me, "Do you think you have the evil eye?" The "evil eye" is a big deal in Greek culture. If someone looks at you with envy or malice, he or she could "give you the evil eye," and you would be cursed. The only way to prevent this was to wear a necklace with a small amulet that looks like an eye: round and blue with a black dot in the middle. And the only way to remove the curse was to find a member in your family (there always seemed to be at least one member in every Greek family) who knew how to mix a special potion and perform a ritual just right. This could be done from afar. My mother said, "Do not worry. Let me call Aunt Ann. She can call Auntie Bessie in California and see what she can do."

About an hour later, my temperature dropped to 101 degrees. Fifteen minutes later, it was 100; 15 minutes after that, it was 99; and in another 15 minutes, my fever completely disappeared. My mother called and asked Tony, "Is Val feeling any better?" When he responded, she replied, "Auntie Bessie said Val had the evil eye and that she would take care of it. I guess she did." Tony and I never took much stock in evil eyes before that, but since that day, I wear my evil eye necklace any time I am going to a social event where there will be a lot of people. You cannot be too careful.

At the start of my eighth month of pregnancy, I woke up one morning with horrible stomach pain and a fever. Of course, I immediately called my mother to see if she could check with Auntie Bessie. No evil eye, the family mystic responded. When my pain grew worse and my fever rose, Dr. Beaver recommended that we meet him at the hospital.

He ran numerous blood tests and then asked me if I had had my appendix out. I had not. He told us that when a woman is pregnant and her symptoms pointed to appendicitis, it still was not certain. So we had two choices: The first option was to operate to see if the problem was my appendix. If it was, there would be a chance that I would go into labor. They would try to stop the labor, but if they could not, the baby had a 10 percent chance of being born premature. I was told that the anesthesia had little chance of hurting the baby; he would just "take a nap" with me. Our second choice was to assume I did not have appendicitis and be treated with antibiotics for an infection instead. However, if I did have appendicitis and my appendix ruptured, the risks to the baby and me would escalate and our chances of a happy outcome would be minimal. So really we had no choice: We would operate.

I was surrounded by doctors, including Dr. Beaver; a general surgeon experienced with appendectomies; a specialist experienced with problem pregnancies; and a neonatal doctor to take care of the baby if he had to be delivered. I was told later that I did, in fact, go into labor, and although I was still asleep and shot up with morphine, I screamed out in pain whenever the monitor showed that I was having a contraction. Tony realized then that the actual delivery might prove quite deafening! I was also told later that when I finally woke up, my first question was, "Did the Celtics win?" It was June 1984, and the Celtics were facing the Lakers in the NBA finals.

I did not deliver Matthew then, and ironically, my appendix was not the cause of my pain. When they saw it was fine, the general surgeon wanted to just close me up. But Dr. Beaver said, "If this poor woman has to endure the pain of this surgery, she should never have to worry about her appendix again. Let us take it out." I was so grateful for that afterward.

The doctors could not figure out exactly what was wrong with me, but after 10 days, I felt well again and went home. But I will never forget leaving the hospital feeling so disheartened, since I had been on the delivery floor surrounded by smiling, happy women taking their babies home. Again my mother saved the day. She bought a teddy bear at the gift shop, wrapped it up in a blanket, and gave it to me to hold as they wheeled me out.

My mother lived with us during the rest of my pregnancy.

Although I was in a lot of pain, it was comforting to have her and Tony for support. Matthew had a horrible habit of kicking me in the place where my surgery had been; my mom would jokingly talk to my stomach and say, "Hey, kiddo. Stop it, or we'll make your life miserable when you come out of there."

One lesson I learned from my experience is that babies are very resilient. During my entire pregnancy with Matthew, I had been so careful about what I ate and drank. I stayed away from caffeine, alcohol, headache medications, and a host of other things that I felt I needed to limit for the health of my baby. Funny that after taking all of those precautions, I had spent time in the hospital shot up with morphine, and Matthew turned out just fine.

As luck would have it, during my eighth month of my pregnancy with my second son, David, I also had severe stomach pains and fever. The first question the doctor in Boston asked me was, "Have you had your appendix out?" When I could emphatically respond, "I definitely have," I was treated with antibiotics. My symptoms disappeared after 10 days. They discovered that I had a rare parasite that became activated when my body was under severe stress, as it was at eight months into pregnancy. That gave us another reason to stop at two children.

Chapter Thirteen
Marriage and Relationships

Tony and I met in an unconventional way. I was working at the Census Bureau in Washington, D.C., and was moving from an apartment in Maryland to an apartment in Virginia. I asked my colleagues if they knew anyone who lived near where I was moving, so that I might join a carpool. I was told that there was a guy down the hall named Tony Roman who lived near there. I nervously walked down the hall, peeked into his office, and asked, "Are you Tony Roman?" When he confirmed that he was, I asked if he was in a carpool that I might be able to join. He replied, "No, but I wouldn't mind starting a carpool with you. However, it would have to be a small carpool, since I only have a two-seater car."

Okay, we had a deal. I was a frugal person who shared an apartment with three other women and drove a Datsun B-210, while Tony lived alone and drove a Triumph Spitfire. The first morning of our carpool, Tony called to say, "I'm sorry, but my car won't start. I guess you'll have to drive."

I responded, "That's okay. I'll be right over." However, when his car stayed in the shop for two weeks, I began to think, "This isn't a carpool. I'm a chauffeur service!" Yet the ride-sharing arrangement worked out, and we became friends. Each morning and evening, we shared our stories. At the time, both Tony and I were in other serious relationships. Both of us were experiencing some relationship problems, so it was helpful for me to get his perspective as a male and for him to get my female perspective. Finally, after many months, Tony asked me, "Why are we putting up with this stuff? Maybe you and I should go on an actual date." The rest is history.

The scary part about changing our relationship was that we both worked at the same place, where a romance could be considered a taboo. But we were attentive to the issue and made sure that it did not become a problem. The wonderful part about changing our relationship was that it was founded upon first being friends.

However, before we got too serious, a key difference between us needed to be addressed. You see, Tony and I met in 1978, and for those of you who are Red Sox fans, you know how horrible a year that was for our team. After choking away a 14½-game lead at the All Star break, the Red Sox ended up losing in a one-game playoff to the dreaded New York Yankees on October 2, 1978. Well, Tony was a Yankee fan. He received so much happiness from his team, while all I ever received was disappointment. I gave him an ultimatum: "Either you become a Red Sox fan or our relationship is over. You need to be as miserable as I am!" One accomplishment I am most proud of is that Tony did become a Red Sox fan. However, I do not know if I can take all the credit: I think all those high-priced free-agent signings by the Yankees general manager, George Steinbrenner, helped out.

Tony and I dated for about three years. I will always

remember the first time Tony brought me to his family's house in Mayfield, Pennsylvania, to meet his mother and sister. They opened the door with big, warm, welcoming smiles on their faces. Since Tony is six feet, one inch tall, I was surprised to see that they were only a couple of inches taller than I was. They gave me huge hugs, and his mother said, "It is so great to meet you, and so nice not to see another tall blonde coming through the door."

> *"Either you become a Red Sox fan or our relationship is over."*

I guess she meant that as a compliment, right?

Tony and I were good friends with a married couple, Paul and Eileen, who had also moved from Boston to Washington. They seemed to get along great together, and we shared a lot of laughs. One night, we all went to one of those mechanical bull bars that were so popular in the late 1970s and early 1980s. You would get on the bull, the man would say, "Start her up!" and then you would ride for about 10 to 30 seconds, until you were thrown off. The man would then say, "Give the guy (or gal) a hand!" Eileen and I knew better and stayed at the table.

Paul and Tony got in line waiting their turns, but did not realize that they were involved in a male competition and the speed of the bull was being accelerated. In front of them was a Marine from Wyoming giving them tips on how to stay on the bull. When it was his turn, the Marine rode the bull like a pro and never fell off. He could have been on the bull forever, so after 30 seconds, the man said "Give the guy a hand!" and the Marine dismounted. Next, it was Tony's turn. When Tony got on the bull, Eileen and I heard "Start her up!" then immediately "Give the guy a hand!" Not only was Tony on the bull the shortest amount of time, but he was catapulted right into the band, past all of the mattresses set up around the bull to cushion riders' falls! He may not have won the time competition, but definitely won in distance! Fortunately, both Tony and the drums survived. Paul then took his turn. He lasted longer but got thrown to the mattresses, and walked back to the table saying, "I'm hurt. I am definitely hurt." We finished our drinks and left.

The next day, the Red Sox were playing the Baltimore Orioles at the old Memorial Stadium in Baltimore, and the four of us had tickets. Tony and I arrived earlier and got to our seats, which were pretty high up. After about 20 minutes, we saw Eileen walking up the stairs to our seats, and right behind her was Paul—on crutches! Eileen, with her dry sense of humor, explained how they had been in the emergency room all night, but refused to let that ruin her chance to see the Red Sox play. Paul, with his equally dry sense of humor, joked about Eileen's total lack of sympathy during the whole ordeal. Yes, they seemed great together, and we had so many laughs that day, retelling the fun events of the previous night. When Tony and I were driving back from the game, I said, "I hope that when we get married, we have a marriage like Paul and Eileen's."

A year later, about one month before our wedding, they informed us that they were getting a divorce. I was devastated and my faith in the concept of marriage was shaken. After all, if they did not make it, how could anyone make it? I learned a lesson from that experience: You never really know what is going on behind closed doors, so focus on your own relationship, instead of envying anyone else's.

Tony and I have now been married for more than 30 years. My personal recipe for a successful marriage is to start with a good sense of humor, and then add flexibility, respect, communication, and planning.

<u>SPORTS AND MARRIAGE</u>

I have often read about how experience in sports can train us for many important life lessons. Here are the marital lessons that popular sports have taught me.

- **Basketball:** Wait for the right moment. Although you should carefully choose the best time to have a difficult conversation, do not wait too long before having the talk. If you have waited 48 hours, you have waited too long.

- **Bicycling:** Know when to change gears. There are times when a decision you made together just does not work out. Do not say "I told you so!" Reevaluate the decision without blaming one another for the mistake.

- **Boxing:** Stay out of the corner. As a married couple, you will have disagreements. Do not hide in a corner, walk on eggshells, or fear rocking the boat. One of the keys to a successful relationship is to figure out how to constructively handle conflict.

- **Camping:** Before you fall asleep, make sure that the campfire is out. Try to work through an argument to a solution and not go to bed angry.

- **Weightlifting:** Set specific goals. Finances are one of the areas in your marriage in which goals are extremely important. Talk with each other about your financial goals, both short-term and long-term.

- **Football:** To reach your goals, you need to work together as a team. Do not sabotage your marriage by thinking too much about yourself and not enough about you as a couple.

- **Golf:** You are never too old. As you approach the second half of your marriage, relish the quiet moments of your empty nest and find ways to enjoy time together again just the two of you.

- **Hockey:** A shootout in hockey is preceded by a two-minute break. When you are having a disagreement, you may need to give each other time and space apart. I am not suggesting separate vacations in the middle of an argument, but giving each other time to gather your thoughts can result in a more productive discussion.

- **Horseback riding:** After a fall, check for injuries and get back on the horse. Figure out why you fell off and avoid making the same mistake. There is no way to avoid making some mistakes in marriage. If you make a mistake, admit it, apologize for it, fix it, and do not repeat it.

Do This for Each Other

- Share the household chores. Since Tony and I have both worked full time professionally with long commutes all of our lives, we share the household duties—doing the laundry, shopping, paying bills, and emptying the dishwasher. Sometimes when relatives from an older generation visit and witness Tony emptying the dishwasher or putting groceries away, they will say to me, "I hope you know how lucky you are to have Tony help out like he does." Those comments are a bit annoying. Yes, I am grateful and happy, but sharing is the way it should be, and I should not have to bow in reverence. After all, is that not what equal rights are all about? Women have the right to participate actively in the workplace, and men have the right to participate actively in the home.

- Give each other a big hug and kiss when you arrive home from work. Spend some time talking together about how the day went.

- Enjoy the experience of just being together. No matter how busy the two of you are, make time for one another. Part of a successful marriage is scheduling date nights, laughing together, relaxing together, and having fun together. It can be as simple as playing a game of Scrabble, going to a movie, or taking a walk together.

- Relish the quiet moments.

- Perform random acts of kindness. Run an errand for your spouse, take care of a task on your spouse's to-do list, or do something special and out of the ordinary.

- Do not be threatened by your spouse's accomplishments. Tell people, especially your spouse, how proud you are of his or her talents and skills.

- Show interest. Interest can be signaled by truly listening and being involved in a conversation. Appropriately timed uh-huhs, nods, and direct eye contact are key signals.

- Be affectionate. You can show affection in subtle ways through acts of tenderness, such as touching or holding hands, or a quick shoulder massage.

- Set aside a time each year for just the two of you to get away, especially when you have kids. Tony and I would plan a long weekend to a wonderfully relaxing place, such as Nantucket, Bermuda, or Bar Harbor, Maine. We always looked forward to that special "alone time" that we guaranteed each other, no matter how hectic things became with the kids.

- Develop traditions. In preparation for my birthday, Tony researches restaurants we have never been to before, and I do not know where we are going until we actually arrive. I do the same for his birthdays. In addition, often instead of buying each other tangible gifts, we buy tickets to a show or ballgame or concert, so that we can share memorable times during that special day.

- When you are flying, instead of each of you having your own piece of luggage, pack some of your things in each suitcase. That way, if a bag is lost, both of you can get by. There is nothing more dangerous to a marriage than your spouse having all of his or her belongings and you having no clothes, no toiletries, nothing!

Say This to Each Other

- Show that you have faith in your mate. Statements such as, "You are doing the right thing" and "I trust your judgment" and "I really value your opinion" should be in your lexis.

- Express your appreciation. Let your spouse know whenever he or she has done something that pleases you.

- Show your concern and be empathetic. Be the shoulder to lean on when your spouse has a problem, is feeling low, or tells you about something distressing or troubling. Be supportive when your spouse is worried. Having empathy requires putting yourself in your spouse's shoes and relating to his or her emotional state. If the problem is at work, remind your spouse of all the other happy parts of his or her life, so that you can maintain balance in your life together.

HANDLE DIFFERENCES OF OPINION

- Identify what you agree on right at the start. That will start the conversation off on a positive note and will eliminate wasted discussion on areas that do not need to be resolved.

- Listen. Focus your attention on what your spouse is saying, instead of planning what you are going to say next.

- Repeat what he or she has said. A good way to ensure you are listening is to repeat back, in a neutral tone, what was just said. "Am I understanding that you feel left out when I work late?" "Are you saying that you do not want to put the boys to bed on Thursday nights?" This calms the discussion down, so that anger does not escalate.

- Fight fair. Each spouse should have the opportunity to explain why he or she is mad, while the other one listens with respect. Argue calmly. Although it inevitably happens sometimes, a loss of control, crying, or yelling makes things worse.

- Be tolerant. At the beginning of a relationship, a person's irritating habits tend to seem unimportant, but over the long term, nightly snoring or monopolizing the remote control can begin to get on your nerves. Acknowledge that some problems cannot be solved, and learn to work around them. No relationship is perfect. Focus on the strengths of your relationship, rather than the annoying inconveniences.

Chapter Fourteen
Organizing the Home

M any of the organizational tactics I have used at the office are also valuable to use at home. For example, the tickler filing system works great for notices, tickets to events, and bills to be paid.

One way I have tried to organize my home life is to look at the things I have to do repeatedly and to then try to automate them. For example, I generally make the same Easter dinner each year. Instead of every year having to think about and write up my plans for that day, I have a Microsoft Excel document that lists every food item I need to have, preparation I need to do, and the time I need to produce each dish. I simply enter the time I want our family to eat, and Excel automatically tells me when to put the turkey and ham in the oven, when to put the potatoes in the oven, cook the vegetables, toss the salad, and heat the bread. I print out the document and place it on the kitchen counter to guide me.

I have a similar technique for packing for trips. I have separate Excel files for a business trip, a family beach trip, and a family winter trip. The file lists all of the items I need to pack, from underwear to casual outfits, to dresses, to toiletries, to umbrellas. I then enter the number of days of my trip, and

Excel automatically fills out how many of each item I should take. This organizational approach helps me not have to think about the same things over and over again.

<u>MANAGE PAPER EFFICIENTLY</u>

- Use folders to create a hierarchy of organization. If you are a den mother, make a folder for your son's Cub Scout pack to store all the papers that are relevant to the Scouts' activities and meetings. Label each folder with a date and title as well.

- Keep a basket on the kitchen counter or hall table where you drop each bill and official paper that arrives in the mail. At a specified time each week, go through them. Pay the bills that are due, and place other papers in your tickler file.

- Keep an area in a file cabinet for warranties. Organize the owner's manuals, warranties, and service agreements in folders and label them, such as Large Appliances, Small Appliances, Computers, and Cars. Staple the original receipt (or a copy if you need the original for tax purposes) to each warranty.

<u>PLAN AHEAD TO SAVE TIME AND HASSLE</u>

- Organize your grocery shopping. Make a list of your favorite brands and regular purchases. Instead of creating a new list each week, store this master list on your computer. If you go to the same grocery store, sort the items by aisle. If not, sort them by category, such as dairy, bakery, and produce. At the bottom of the list, leave a blank area. Print and keep the list on your refrigerator and invite your family to add items to this list. If the item becomes a favorite, add it to the master list. When you are ready to go to the grocery store, cross out the regular purchases that you do not have to buy on that trip. Paper clip or staple to the list the coupons for items that you plan to buy. When shopping, make a note of the aisle where the newly added items are located. After returning, be sure to update your master list.

• Organize your holiday shopping. Create a spreadsheet and list everyone on your gift list in one column. Be sure to include recipients such as your hairdresser and newspaper carriers. Use the second column to list gift ideas for that person, the third column to record actual gifts purchased, and the fourth column to record the amounts spent. As you shop and purchase the gifts listed, update your spreadsheet by moving the gift idea to the gifts purchased column and adding the price paid to the amounts spent column. You can avoid giving duplicate gifts by checking the spreadsheets from previous years. Other suggestions include:

   o Keep an envelope for the receipts and write the name of the gift recipient on the back of each.

   o Pick up a few generic gifts, such as bottles of wine, candles, or boxes of chocolates, for those people who give you a gift unexpectedly. Record these gifts by adding a few lines to your spreadsheet and keep a total in the amounts spent column, so that you are aware of your spending.

   o Although online retailers charge for gift-wrapping and shipping, consider shipping the gift directly to the recipient. It may end up being cheaper than the costs

of shipping it to your home, wrapping it yourself, and then shipping it to the recipient.

o Shop for holiday gifts all year, instead of waiting until the season. This will make your presents more interesting for the recipient and you will not collapse under the weight of shopping overload. Shop for gifts while on vacation, such as scarves while in France and jewelry while in Greece.

CONTROL STORAGE

- Use clear plastic boxes to store things, so you can see inside without having to open the box.

- When you move, color-code your boxes with self-stick dots. Use one colored dot for the boxes that go to the kitchen, another colored dot for the office, another colored dot for the garage, and so on. Before moving day, go to your new residence and place corresponding colored dots on the walls of the appropriate rooms.

- When packing boxes for moving or storage, label them three times—on one short side, on one long side, and on the top. That way, no matter how you have to stack or set the boxes up, you can see which box is which.

- When moving, pack heavy items, like books, in a rolling suitcase. Boxes are hard to carry and tend to tear when they are too heavy.

- Keep linen sets together. For each set of sheets, put the top and bottom sheet with one of the pillowcases together and store them in the matching pillow case.

- Store smaller pieces of luggage inside larger pieces of luggage.

- Cut open toilet paper rolls and use as a cuff to stop rolls of wrapping paper from unrolling.

- Place a paper clip at the end of a roll of tape to prevent it from sticking to the roll, allowing you to find the start of the tape easily.

- Color-code your keys by applying a thick coat of a different shade of nail polish to the top of each one.

- Store items you take with you regularly in the car trunk. For example, in the summer, leave beach chairs and tennis equipment in the car. In the autumn, stow a jacket; in the spring, an umbrella. For winter, keep the salt and shovel in the trunk.

- Place a hanging shoe rack on the back of a door to store cleaning supplies and keep them up away from the kids.

- Magnetize your medicine cabinet. Mount a long magnet along the back of your medicine cabinet to hold tweezers, clippers, little scissors, and other small metal objects.

- Keep all your take-out menus in a single place. Write the date on the menus. Cull the collection at the end of each year, so that you are not keeping menus from places that have closed or you do not patronize anymore.

- Have your children help you get things done before bedtime. This could include picking up toys, laying out tomorrow's clothes, and collecting anything they will need for school and putting it by the door.

- Create a schedule for routine household chores. Give your children the chance to choose the tasks they prefer and the times by which they will complete them. Include yourself and your husband in the chart. Tell your children that if they have conflicts because of sports practices or school projects, they can negotiate with other family members to swap to get tasks done.

- Train your children so that when they take a phone message, they repeat the spelling of the caller's name and phone number to the caller to ensure accuracy.

- Place folded garbage bags at the bottom of your trash cans, under the garbage bag that is open and in use. When you fill and remove that one, the next bag is already there!

- Give each member of the family his or her own lingerie bag to store their dirty socks and underwear. Put these entire bags in the washer and dryer, so that they are quick and easy to sort when they are clean and dry.

- Cut down snow-shoveling time, which is very important to those of us who live in New England. Spread vegetable shortening over the blade of your shovel to create a water-resistant seal that will keep the snow from sticking to it. Then you will not have to stop every few minutes to clean off the snow buildup.

- Keep a stash of all-purpose greeting cards and note cards at home. These should include get-well, birthday, sympathy, and thank-you cards.

- Keep doubles and triples of things you use all the time (scissors, tape, reading glasses, cleaning supplies) and store them in various places around your house. This will save you extra trips to the store and extra trips up and down the stairs.

- Looking for particular items that you want to try to get at yard sales? Instead of looking through all of the newspapers for local yard sales each weekend, check out the website www.yardsaletreasuremap.com. Enter your city and the types of items you are looking for, such as exercise equipment, and it will show you where the closest yard sales are for those items.

- For speedy furniture painting or varnishing, pull on a rubber glove and then pull an old sock over that. Dip your covered hand in the paint or varnish and use it to coat the furniture. Your fingers will easily be able to reach every crevice and curve and will cut the time in half. Time saved on cleanup is even better. Instead of having to wash paint brushes, just take the sock and glove off and throw them away.

- Cut lawn-mowing time by spraying the mower's blades with cooking spray before you begin. The oil acts as a nonstick coating, which helps prevent clogs by allowing the grass to slide right off.

Chapter Fifteen
Parenting Pointers

When my son, Matthew, was in fourth grade, our town had split the fourth graders into two bus schedule groups. Half of the fourth graders went on the bus with the kindergarten through third graders, and the other half took the bus with the fifth through eighth graders. Matthew was assigned to the one with the fifth through eighth graders. The evening after Matthew's first day on the bus, he asked me, "Mom, am I a Virgil?"

I did not know what to say, so I quickly responded, "Matthew, you are a Roman." He let it go at that, but each evening he came home with another "What does this [sexually associated] word mean?" question, getting more worrisome each day.

I told him that if he heard a word he did not understand, it was very important for him to ask us about it, since he could get himself into trouble if he used a word incorrectly. He continued to ask, and the words he asked about continued to increase in intensity. I soon realized that we had to have "The Talk" sooner than I thought. So that weekend I took him out for a drive. I found that talking in the car with the absence of eye contact seemed to make both of us feel more comfortable. I explained sex and answered his questions honestly and directly.

A few weeks later, Matthew asked, "Mom, what is a diaphragm?" Oh my God, I thought, he is only in fourth grade! But I took a deep breath and proceeded to tell him about birth control. "Do you remember a while ago that we talked about how a mom and dad love each other, and how they can share their love with each other, and how sometimes a baby can be made?" Matthew shook his head in agreement, so I continued. "Well, sometimes the mom and dad are not ready to have a baby, so the mom can go to the doctor and get something called a diaphragm." As I continued to provide more details, I noticed that Matthew had a very puzzled look on his face. I could tell he was thinking hard; after all, this was a hard concept to comprehend. Finally, he said in a somewhat disbelieving tone, "Mom, that cannot be right."

I resumed my explanation, and he again said, "Mom, that just cannot be right." I asked him why he thought that, and he responded, "Because my music teacher says I have to breathe through it!" I learned that day to ask for more clarification before answering a question.

"Mom, what is a diaphragm?"

My, how different Matthew's experience was from mine when it came to learning and talking about sex. After I had been horrified at the arrival of my first period, my mother decided it must be time to have "The Talk." She spoke with her friend, who was a devout Catholic, and borrowed her church's educational program on the subject. My father left the house. My mother asked me to come into the living room, a room that we never used. She closed the door behind us and asked me to sit on a couch, a couch where I had never sat. She went to the record player and put on an album. She returned with a book and sat down with me on the couch. She opened the first page and there was a picture of a penis. The album's narrator said, "This is a penis." We then heard a beep and my mother turned the page. We proceeded to go through each page of the book at the pace of the album's comments and beeps. When the album finished, she closed the book and told me that if I had any questions later, to let her know. We both left the room. I still smile each time I remember that night.

Sex was a very difficult topic for my mother to discuss. Once after Tony and I were engaged, I drove up from Washington to spend Christmas with my family. Tony went to Pennsylvania to spend the holiday with his family. The day after I arrived, I developed what I thought to be a yeast infection. My mother spoke with her doctor and was able to make an appointment for me.

After the doctor examined me, he told me that he thought I had a sexually transmitted disease. When I told him that I was engaged and was only sexually active with my fiancé, he replied, "Well, maybe he is not as loyal to you as you are to him." He next asked me if I had been out of the state over the past 48 hours. Of course I had: I had driven up the east coast from Washington, D.C., the day before. He then told me that legally he would have to notify all the states I had driven through that I most likely had a sexually transmitted disease. I could not believe it! He was going to notify Virginia, Maryland, Delaware, New Jersey, New York, Connecticut, Massachusetts, and New Hampshire that I had carried a sexually transmitted disease through their states? I was horrified. Was I having a nightmare? Was I in an episode of *Candid Camera*? He told me he would get the results of my lab test within the next three days. I would have to go through all of Christmas Eve and Christmas Day not knowing what was happening.

When I came out of the doctor's office, my mother asked me what was wrong, and after hearing the story, she was devastated. We would all feel the shame and embarrassment of others knowing I was sexually active. I would become a one-person national health crisis.

When I arrived back at my parents' house, I called Tony. I said in a whispered voice, "I promise I will not get mad, but you have to tell me the absolute truth. Have you been with anyone else?" To which he immediately responded, "Of course not." After I explained my predicament, he calmed me down, telling me that I most likely had a yeast infection as originally thought, not to worry, and to enjoy Christmas. Yeah, right. It was the worst Christmas ever.

The day after Christmas, I called the doctor's office to get the lab results. The nurse said that, indeed, I had a yeast infection and that the doctor had called in a prescription for me. Obviously, I was ecstatic with the news, but why did I have to go through all that stress? When I think back on this traumatic experience, I wonder whether the doctor was an absolute quack or whether my mother had somehow put him up to it, so that I would never consider pre-marital sex again! (My money is on the quack.)

We all know that once we have children, our lives are never the same. We are barraged with constantly changing challenges. One of the biggest lessons I learned is that you do not have to be a perfect parent to be a great parent. Accepting this reality takes enormous pressure off of you. If you try to be the super-mother who does everything right, you will always be guilt-ridden, stressed, and exhausted, and will miss out on the enjoyment of the journey.

Although it can be tough and sometimes you think you will never get through a particular problem, challenge, or phase, there are so many wonderful, rewarding times that make it all worthwhile. Also, the funny experiences can make you giggle for a lifetime. Here are some other lessons I learned.

PREPARE TO BE EMBARRASSED

When my son David was about four years old, we were in church one Sunday when the priest said, "Here is a reading according to the Romans." David jumped up and yelled out to the congregation, "That's us! That's us!" Although embarrassing, people definitely remembered who we were!

<u>DEAL WITH FOUL LANGUAGE</u>

One night, when David was in first grade, he said, "Today, Connor said a bad word at school." I asked him what it was, and he whispered, "It is a four letter word and it starts with an F." Tony and I looked at each other, wondering if it was what we thought it was, and if so, how awful it was for David to hear it in the first grade. Then David blurted out, "Connor said the word 'fart.'" We were so relieved, trying not to laugh. However, I had to take some of the blame for his reaction. I had never liked the word "fart," so I always used the phrase "air poop" with the kids. David probably thought that the word "fart" was bad.

<u>TEACH TEENS TO DRIVE</u>

When Matthew tested for his driver's license, he easily passed the written test and then went out for the driving portion. When the instructor told Matthew to take a left near our church, at an intersection separated by a traffic island, he took a left on the wrong side of the island and immediately failed the test. The next day, our town put a sign at that fork that said "Do Not Enter," which we have affectionately called Matthew's Sign ever since. Matthew took the test again and did get his license, jokingly saying, "If we had gone to church more often, I might have passed the test the first time!"

I took Matthew out to learn how to drive and enjoyed the experience. When David was ready to learn to drive, I thought that I would provide equal time with him. For his first lesson, I turned the car around in the driveway, so he could just drive out and not have to back up. We went over all of the dashboard instruments, where they were and what they did. I could tell that David was very eager to begin. When I said, "Now, slowly press down on the gas pedal," for some unknown reason, he gunned it. We tore down the driveway, across the road, and into the neighbor's yard. Thankfully, he obeyed my "HIT THE

BRAKE!" directive. We stopped, I returned to the driver's seat, and I was able to catch my breath while I backed the car out of the neighbor's yard.

When David got back into the driver's seat and proceeded to drive slowly down our road, my heart began to resume a normal beat. When I instructed him to take a left onto a nearby cul-de-sac, he did so with confidence and care. I, too, became more confident that this lesson was now on the right track and going well. We went around the cul-de-sac and came to the stop sign where we planned to take a left back onto the main road. I am not sure whether it was due to eagerness or overconfidence or nerves, but David pulled the steering wheel sharply to the left and gunned the gas pedal again. In that cul-de-sac, we became a teacup ride at Disney World!

That was it. I lost my cool and told David to stop and let me drive the car home. We both got out of the car. I moved into the driver's seat, but he would not get back into the car. I asked, "Would you please get back into the car?" and he emphatically answered, "No, I will walk home!" I asked again, but again he refused. Since we were only about a quarter-mile from the house, I drove off.

Tony has a different version of the event. He tells the story, "I saw them drive off. About five minutes later, I see Val driving the car home. She is alone. No David. I knew this could not be good."

When David returned home, we apologized to each other and agreed that it might be best for Dad to do the teaching for a while. After a few months, when I regained my courage and David's driving abilities improved, I resumed my teaching role. We still laugh about that first lesson. Although over the years there were some tough times and various tests of my patience and fortitude, taking a role in my sons' learning how to drive, which is such an important milestone in life, meant a lot to me and to them, too. I am grateful that I was able to do it.

CHAPTER FIFTEEN: PARENTING POINTERS

<u>Teach Gender Equality</u>

I am not sure if it was thanks to my parents' encouragement, my education at Wellesley College, or my work experience in Washington, D.C., but I am especially committed to gender equality. I wanted my two sons to grow up with the same commitment. Their pediatrician was a woman, and I often read storybooks to them that portrayed girls and women in a positive light. When I made up bedtime stories, my sons often heard me say things like, "There once was a doctor, and her name was Dr. Jones" or "There was a police officer, and her name was Officer Smith." In conversations, I replaced words like "fireman" with "firefighter" and "mailman" with "mail carrier." I thought I had done a pretty good job, until David came home from school when he was in third grade and said, "Katie was stupid today. She said she wanted to be a doctor, but everyone told her she could only be a nurse." I was disappointed that he did not speak out on her behalf. I proceeded to remind him that his doctor was a grown-up girl and that Katie, like he, could be anything she wanted to be. I learned that day that sometimes outside forces are so strong that we have to make extra efforts to overcome them.

<u>Make the Most of It</u>

When I became a mother, friends and relatives would say, "Enjoy every minute," or "Savor every experience," or "It passes so quickly." Good advice! I did enjoy every minute and savor every experience, and sure enough, time did pass quickly. I was lucky to realize when my boys were still young that there is a very brief time when you are the most important person to them. All young children want to spend time with their parents. When they become teenagers, their lives expand and a parent's role is lessened. When my children were young and wanted (and demanded) much of my time, I tried not to lose sight of the fact that this was not going to last very long—a dozen years at the most. It is so important to realize this fact as early as you can, so that you can cherish your time together.

Looking back, although there were times when I felt tired or dreaded the rain or the cold, I am so glad that I attended every soccer, baseball, and basketball game and tennis match that my sons played. They provided me with a lifetime of memories. I must admit, however, that I cunningly discouraged our kids from playing football and hockey. In New England, winter sports are particularly demanding on parents, as well as on children. Who wants to be on a football field in November in New England or drive to a hockey practice at 5 a.m. on a Sunday, the only rink time available?

Look to the next page for a poem that had a special impact on me that I would like to share with you. *The Last Time,* credited to Taryn McLean, is about motherhood, and I hope that it may have a positive impact on you, too.

PLAN FAMILY VACATIONS WISELY

One thing I did to increase family togetherness was to make it attractive for my sons to want to come on family vacations. I planned vacations around their interests. For our family, sports teams and events are important. The boys played sports, and we are all big Boston sports fans. Therefore, I planned traditional family vacations around the Red Sox. Each year, I asked my sons if they were interested in joining me and their dad for another Red Sox trip, and to my delight, they always took me up on the invitation. It was a great (and a bit sneaky) way to get the family together.

When the kids were young, we would travel down to Florida to enjoy spring training for a week. As the boys went around getting autographs from their favorite players, Tony and I sat in the stands, newspapers in hand, basking in the

THE LAST TIME

From the moment you hold your baby in your arms, you will never
    be the same.
You might long for the person you were before,
When you had freedom and time,
And nothing in particular to worry about.
You will know tiredness like you never knew it before,
And days will run into days that are exactly the same,
Full of feeding and burping,
Whining and fighting,
Naps, or lack of naps.
It might seem like a never-ending cycle.
But don't forget...
There is a last time for everything.
There will come a time when you will feed your baby for the very
    last time.
They will fall asleep on you after a long day
And it will be the last time you ever hold your sleeping child.
One day you will carry them on your hip, then set them down,
And never pick them up that way again.
You will scrub their hair in the bath one night
And from that day on they will want to bathe alone.
They will hold your hand to cross the road,
Then never reach for it again.
They will creep into your room at midnight for cuddles,
And it will be the last night you ever wake for this.
One afternoon you will sing "The Wheels on the Bus" and do all the
    actions,
Then you'll never sing that song again.
They will kiss you goodbye at the school gate,
The next day they will ask to walk to the gate alone.
You will read a final bedtime story and wipe your last dirty face.
They will one day run to you with arms raised, for the very last time.
The thing is, you won't even know it's the last time until there are no
    more times, and even then, it will take you a while to realize.
So while you are living in these times, remember there are only so
    many of them and when they are gone, you will yearn for just
    one more day of them
For one last time.

sunshine. In the summer, we would select a city where the Red Sox were playing. I bought tickets for the games and tried to make reservations in the same hotel where the players were staying. We became groupies for a few days with thousands of other members of Red Sox Nation! In this way, we toured many different places and did some great sightseeing, including the Grand Canyon through an Arizona Diamondbacks series; Los Angeles through an Angels series; the San Francisco Bay area through an Oakland Athletics series; and Niagara Falls through a Toronto Blue Jays series.

Other families we knew traveled to countries where their children could practice the language skills they were learning in school; catch shows on Broadway or at the Kennedy Center; or visit the sites of the kids' favorite books and movies, such as the Harry Potter tour of London or the Huck Finn cruise down the Mississippi.

DEVELOP YOUR OWN FAMILY TRADITIONS

As in the case of our annual Red Sox trips, I have loved creating traditions. I guess that comes from my Greek heritage, which is so steeped in tradition. One of my favorite family traditions happens the Wednesday before Thanksgiving. When the boys were very young, I had that day off from the City of Cambridge. Tony did not have the day off from his job, so Matthew, David, and I would go to a children's movie. We frequently went to a place called Chunky's, which had tables where we could sit, order off the menu, and watch the movie—a children's version of a dinner theater! Every year, that is how we spent the Wednesday afternoon before Thanksgiving.

As the years passed, I always asked Matthew and David if they wanted to go again, and whether they wanted to see a regular movie instead of a children's movie. To my surprise, the tradition of seeing a children's movie together each year seemed to mean as much to them as it did to me, so our old tradition continued. Although Matthew has moved to Los Angeles, David and I still go to the movies, and Matthew always wants to know which children's movie we plan to see. We continue to be the oldest people in the theater, but that is part of the fun!

Tony has created traditions, too. Each Easter, he hides plastic eggs in the front and back yards. When the kids were very young, the eggs contained pieces of candy or small toys and were fairly easy to find. However, as the kids got older, Tony expanded the hunt into a treasure hunt. Inside one of the eggs hidden in the yard was a clue that would bring the kids to a location inside the house. There they would find one of the next 12 clues Tony had hidden. The clues could relate to literature, to past experiences, or to items in the house. An example might be, "Pierre has your next clue and he doesn't care." In a bookshelf upstairs was their childhood book entitled *Pierre*, by Maurice Sendak, and the clue inside the book would send them to the next clue. The clues ultimately led to a hidden pirate's chest that contained the treasure. When we started this tradition, the treasure was a $1 bill; it has since gone up to $20! No matter how old our sons get, they still look forward to Dad's Easter Egg Hunt. In fact, since Matthew moved to Los Angeles, we use video conferencing, either through Skype or FaceTime. I follow David with the laptop, so that Matthew can experience what David experiences and also actively participate.

As soon as the kids could walk, we began the tradition of going to the library every Saturday. Matthew and David would pick out seven children's books—one for each day of the week. We would read them

together and then go back the next Saturday and exchange them for seven more. I do believe that this ritual played a big part in my sons' love for reading, as well as their ability to read at a younger than average age.

As a child, I enjoyed playing Sorry with my mother at the kitchen table. I wanted my sons to also have fond memories of playing board games together. We started with Candyland and Chutes and Ladders, progressed to Sorry, and moved on to Boggle, Trivial Pursuit, and Scattergories. To this day, when we are all together for the holidays, we still enjoy sitting at the kitchen table and playing Boggle, Scattergories, or Scrabble.

I also found that developing a traditional family phrase helped my children remember important points. For example, I always told the kids when they went out, "Be Smart. Be Safe." That covered a wide range of disciplinary topics and let them know that I trusted their good judgment. It got to the point that I only had to look at them as they left the house and they would say, "Be Smart. Be Safe. Do not worry, Mom." To this day, they remember that phrase.

DEAL WITH DAY CARE

The search for day care was one of the most stressful activities I experienced as a parent. I never had the feeling that the day care situation was settled for good; it frequently needed to change to adjust to new circumstances. I had no relatives who lived nearby who could help out, and when I look back on the more than 20 years of day care that I had to arrange, I am still amazed at how I was successfully able to patch things together. I used formal day care centers, home-based day care centers, and day care providers who came to my home. Each had its special value.

I had to return to work when my first son was six months old. I took him to a local small home-based day care. Matthew received a lot of close, individual attention, yet had the opportunity to interact with one or two other children. One of the children was slightly older than Matthew, so that provided Matthew with an added learning opportunity. I maintained that arrangement for almost a year.

When we moved to New Hampshire, I debated whether to find him day care near home or near work, which was over an hour away. I chose day care near work. Matthew was able to sleep in the car during the morning commute. By choosing a day care center near work, I could pick him up without getting stuck in traffic. This saved me the worry of paying for extra time if I had to sit in a rush-hour jam, and Matthew knew exactly when I would be picking him up. We spent a lot of time in traffic once I picked him up, but we could talk or sing together while we waited. Sometimes we stopped at a park or a restaurant on the way home.

When my second son was born, Matthew was four years old and attending a local pre-school. We hired a babysitter to watch David at home. Having somebody come to the house can be expensive, but if you have more than one child, it can be cost effective. In my case, the babysitter had a car, so she could pick up Matthew after preschool. The kids could stay in their familiar surroundings. The convenience for me and the stability for the children made it worth the expense.

Once David started preschool, I hired Melinda Ouellette, a teacher who could provide after-school care, and fortunately, summer care as well. When she moved away for a couple of years, I hired high school and college students to fill in. But thankfully, Melinda returned to our local school system and could pick up where she left off. Melinda was part of our day care arrangements for more than 12 years, taking one or both of our boys to afternoon karate classes, soccer practices, and other activities.

Having Melinda in our family's life was and still is a gift. Most people are not as fortunate to have such a long-term relationship. In fact, Melinda was the Confirmation sponsor for both of our sons, and although everyone is grown up, we are still very close. She married and has a daughter, Jessie Rose, for whom I now babysit!

In between these arrangements, I had some techniques for scrambling for day care. For summer day care, I looked locally. I let the neighbors and school teachers know I was looking for babysitters.

Many high school and college students, especially those who already know you, appreciate having a job nearby. Sometimes when I asked teachers for recommendations, they surprised me by offering to work themselves. I also posted the job on local college bulletin boards. Today most colleges have job postings online. It can pay to call the education or childhood development departments at colleges to see if there is someone interested.

I have determined that putting my children in day care was fine, not damaging as some people may assert. In fact, my children enjoyed the interaction with other children and developed social skills at an early age. The routine of day care provided stability and consistency at the same time it provided a change of scenery and different toys. Some people have tried to impose guilt on me, but I am confident that day care was a good choice. I also know that the time I did have to spend with my children was put to good use—I chose quality over quantity.

<u>KEEP YOUR KIDS HEALTHY AND SAFE</u>

- How much sleep each night does your child need? According to the National Sleep Foundation, toddlers need 12 to 14 hours, preschoolers need 11 to 13 hours, school-age children need 10 to 11 hours, adolescents need 9 to 10 hours, and adults need 7 to 9 hours.

- Set your water heater no higher than 120 degrees Fahrenheit to avoid scalding.

- Show your child how to begin to brush his teeth as soon as they come in. Take your child to the dentist starting with his first birthday. Use fluoride-free toothpaste until your baby is old enough to rinse his mouth.

- What percentile is your child in? Find out where your child stands in relation to his or her peers by consulting a standardized developmental tool online. I found the Ages and Stages questionnaire available on the University of Oregon website (asq.uoregon.edu) helpful. Many times parents are concerned about developmental delays that are absolutely normal.

- Does your infant get frequent ear infections? Try feeding the bottle to her when she is upright and her head is elevated, instead of when she is lying down.

- To treat a cough in a child over a year old, give him a teaspoon of honey. A Penn State Children's Hospital study compared giving a teaspoon of buckwheat honey, a honey-flavored cough suppressant, or no treatment to 105 children with upper respiratory tract infections, and found that honey worked best at calming coughs.

- Be certain to change the batteries in your smoke detectors once a year. Check them in the fall and spring when you change the time of your clocks.

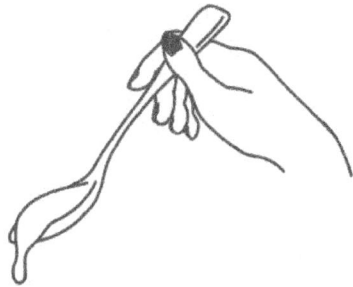

- Put child safety latches on bathroom cupboards and cabinets. Any medicine or cream is a potential poison to a young child.

- Place plug protectors in all unused electrical outlets.

- Raise and secure cords for blinds and drapes.

- Dirty toys? You would be surprised how many of them you can load in the dishwasher. You can simply sterilize them without adding soap, or if they are really dirty, use regular dishwasher detergent. Many plush toys can be washed on the gentle cycle of your washing machine.

- Place a foam swimming pool "noodle" inside the edge of a fitted sheet to prevent your child from rolling out of bed.

- Put stuffed animals or a plush snake along a windowsill to keep out drafts.

- Keep a couple of pepper packets in your purse. When your child gets a scrape, shake the pepper onto the cleaned area. The small specs coagulate the blood, the antibacterial properties prevent infection, and it does not sting. Rinse after five minutes.

KEEP ORGANIZED

- Color-coordinate your home wall calendar. Use a different color pen for each child, for you, and for your spouse. That way, you will also have a visual view of whether the month is especially busy for certain family members.

- Use loose-leaf binders to hold schoolwork and drawings, organized by year, for each child. In addition to keeping things organized, your child can easily access past work and recognize the progress he has made. You can purchase plastic inserts at office supply stores, so that you can save small items, such as leaves or small drawings.

- Use newspaper or old maps for wrapping gifts. The comics work well for a child's birthday gift, as do the sports pages for sports lovers.

Chapter Sixteen
The Cooking Conundrum

M y mother was a great cook. So was her mother. I do not cook. In fact, I occasionally check my oven for cobwebs!

I could cook, but I do not want to spend the time that cooking takes. I figure my mother spent four hours a day shopping, cooking, setting the table, and clearing up. I do not have that kind of time. When my kids were young, I spent four hours a week to make dinner on Sunday, which we called Family Dinner. I also hosted Easter dinner and Christmas Eve dinner each year. The rest of our meals were generally takeout, eating at a restaurant, or being guests of other family members and friends.

When I ask the hostess of an upcoming dinner what she would like me to bring, and she asks me what my specialty is, I generally respond, "It is anything I can purchase in a bakery, so how about I bring a dessert?"

Now I have to address two of the most difficult cooking-related topics in my life: those darn cookie swaps and those dreams of my family sitting down at the table each evening for a delicious home-cooked meal!

In 1986, we moved to Windham, New Hampshire, a small

affluent town. Our neighborhood was filled with people our age with young kids. In December of that year, I was invited to the neighborhood cookie swap. I had never been to a cookie swap and I rarely made cookies. However, I thought it was a great opportunity to meet people. "Just bring six dozen cookies and a container to bring six dozen cookies home," the hostess instructed.

Six dozen cookies! I was nervous. After all, making cookies in general was difficult for me. Once a few years back, I had decided to try to make chocolate peanut butter balls for Christmas. For me, working with peanut butter turned out to be a horror, a "one and done" activity. Somehow, the wooden spoon and my fingers got into a brawl with the electric mixer. Pain shot through my hand, and a string of curse words shot out of my mouth. This was happening just as my husband was opening the door to greet Christmas carolers, and my husband jokingly said, "Ahh, the sounds of the holidays."

Making the required six dozen cookies for the cookie swap was painful, but I powered through it. I made my chocolate chip cookies from a recipe off the back of a bag of chocolate chips. I was stirring up yet another batch of cookie batter, and Matthew, my two-year-old, was sitting on the counter next to me to observe. I heard him say in his sweet little voice, "I love you."

I looked at him and said, "I love you too, honey."

He responded, again in his sweet little voice, "I was talking to the cookies."

I brought my cookies and the required container to my neighbor's guest-filled home, palatial and beautifully decorated for the holiday season, and was greeted at the door with a warm, "Welcome to the neighborhood, Valerie. We are so glad you could come!" The women were all smiles, and laughter filled the house. The hostess brought me over to a group of guests and said, "This is Valerie Roman. She just moved into the neighborhood from Virginia and she works in Cambridge."

Throughout the evening, I was frequently introduced as, "This is Valerie. She is the one who works full time in Cambridge."

I was frequently asked, "How do you do it—all that commuting and working full time?"

Then the hostess came over to me and said, "Valerie, come with me, I want you to meet someone else who also works."

She took me over to a woman and said, "This is Valerie. She works, like you do."

Odd introduction, but my spirits rose a bit, and I asked the woman about her work. She asked, "Isn't it amazing how so many of the women in this neighborhood don't work? I can't imagine not being as busy as I am."

I asked her what she did, and she responded, "I volunteer at the senior center on Tuesday and Thursday mornings." Oh, you have got to be kidding me! I thought. I went home that evening depressed a bit, thinking, "How do these women who all live in gorgeous houses not work professionally, while my husband and I work full time to make ends meet?" I was even more depressed about the fact that I had the worst cookies there!

I was reminded of the movie *The Stepford Wives*, in which the women were beautiful, extremely happy, and calm; they kept their homes impeccably clean and organized; and were the best cooks. Oh no, I was allowing the Donna Reed Syndrome to drag me into yet another media-driven depiction of the perfect woman!

I still attend the annual cookie swaps. When my boys were young, each time I returned, they would say, "This is great. You bake those boring cookies and come back with all these great cookies!" We have downsized the group to about a dozen people, and the older I get, the more fun I have. However, my cookies have not gotten much better!

The second most difficult cooking-related topic in my life is my dream of my family sitting down at the table each evening for a delicious home-cooked meal, just as I had done as a child. I was once on a business trip, and a Wellesley College friend of mine invited me to her house. Matthew and David were about seven and three years of age, respectively, and my friend had three sons, about the same ages as my boys, with another one in the middle. I walked into her house and immediately noticed the pure white walls and carpeting and the calming classical music in the background. Visions of my noisy home with my juice-stained rugs and my kids running around came over me. Her three sons walked over to me and said hello. My friend introduced me and then suggested that the boys go upstairs and read a bit before dinner, saying, "Remember, it is Mom's quiet time with her friend."

My friend asked me if I was hungry for dinner and I responded, "I hope you did not cook. Let us just order pizza or some Chinese."

She said, "Oh no. Tonight we will have chicken l'orange. That is the menu for the third Thursday of the month."

I laughed, thinking she was kidding, and asked, "You do not cook like this every night, do you?"

She responded, "Of course. I have this menu book that plans out all of our family meals." She took out a steno notebook and began to read, "For the third week of each month: Monday our dinner is steak with madeira mushroom sauce, wild rice, and braised vegetable medley; Tuesday it's chicken Florentine with curried couscous pilaf and green beans amandine; Wednesday it's veal parmigiana, with tortellini and salad. Don't you have a book like this?"

I laughed and said, "Yes, but mine says, 'Monday is pizza, Tuesday is Chinese, Wednesday is Burger King, and so on.'"

A few years ago, I asked my son, David, "Tell me the truth. Do you ever wish we had more home-cooked dinners?" He quickly responded, "Heck no." In fact, he responded so quickly that I was not sure if he was critiquing my cooking! But I have thought about it and come to the conclusion (or should I say absolution): For me, since I worked full time professionally and had a long commute, instead of spending what little time I had left in the evening cooking in the kitchen, I chose to spend that time talking with Tony and the kids, either at the dinner table enjoying a take-out meal or at a local restaurant. No prepping, no cooking, no cleanup—just face time. For me, it was the right decision.

Throughout the years, I did learn a few tips about cooking and handling food that I will pass along.

- Bread a bit stale and you need to make a quick sandwich? Sprinkle slices with water and microwave them for 30 seconds.

- Lemons too firm to juice? Microwave them on high for 10 seconds and roll them hard against the counter to loosen up their pulp. Repeat for as many times as needed.

- When boiling corn on the cob, add a pinch of sugar to help bring out the corn's natural sweetness.

- Put a wooden spoon across a pot of water to keep it from boiling over.

- Use a pizza cutter instead of a knife to cut brownies in the baking pan.

- After draining hardboiled eggs, return them to the pot, put the lid on, shake gently to crack the shells, add ice water to the pan, soak for two minutes, then peel.

- When reheating leftovers in the microwave, scrape out an empty space in the middle so they will heat up more evenly.

- When you reheat pizza in the microwave, put a small amount of water in a glass alongside it to keep the crust from getting chewy.

- Use a muffin tin to easily serve condiments at a barbeque. It will also help you cut down on dish washing.

- Freeze coffee in an ice cube tray, so when you make an iced coffee, the frozen coffee cubes do not water down the coffee.

- Freeze several different sizes of water bottles to keep food chilled in an ice chest. When the water melts, you can drink it!

Now, I will admit that the title of this chapter might seem dishonest. You probably expected more recipes, didn't you? After all these years of cookie swaps, I offer here the easiest and most flexible recipe I know—the Cake-Mix Cookie. One of my favorite combinations is dark chocolate fudge cake mix with Andes mint baking chips.

Cake-Mix Cookies

Ingredients:
One box (18¼ ounces) of any flavor cake mix
2 eggs
½ cup of vegetable oil
A bag of chocolate chips, M&M's, or another add-in

Directions:
Mix the four ingredients in a bowl. Form into balls and bake at 350 degrees for 8-9 minutes. Cool in the pan a few minutes before removing.

Yield:
Makes 36 delicious home-baked cookies!

Chapter Seventeen
Cleaning Tips

When I returned home to complete my difficult pregnancy with Matthew, my husband and I decided to hire someone to clean our house on a temporary basis. That was more than 30 years ago. Once we did it, we could never go back. If you have the financial means to do so, hire a cleaning service. Life is too busy; if you can use the time that you would have spent cleaning, and do something else that is meaningful—playing with your kids, reading a book, or going out with friends—it is well worth the expense.

The Soap and Detergent Association (yes, believe it or not, there is one) found that 77 percent of Americans reported that they participate in the spring-cleaning ritual. For us 23 percent who do not participate in this ritual, here are some other ideas and shortcuts.

Tips for the Bathroom

- Tie a plastic bag of vinegar around a shower head for 24 hours to remove built-up residue and to increase water pressure.

- Clean a plastic shower curtain and liner by putting them into the washing machine with a bath towel or two for scrubbing action, along with the usual amount of detergent. Then place them in the dryer for a couple of minutes or hang to dry.

- Keep a bathroom mirror from fogging up by spreading a little shaving cream on it and then wiping it down.

- Use newspaper to wipe away tough streaks on windows and mirrors.

Tips for the Kitchen

- Run your metal sink strainer through the dishwasher to kill germs and bacteria that collect in it.

- Sharpen the blades on your garbage disposal by running ice cubes through it.

- Place a towel in the bottom of the kitchen sink to prevent china and crystal from breaking when you wash them.

- Use ketchup to remove tarnish from copper and brass cookware. Squeeze ketchup onto a cloth and rub it onto the pots and pans. They should go back to their coppery color in minutes. Rinse with warm water and dry with a towel.

- Use club soda to shine up a stainless steel sink. Buff with a cloth dampened with club soda, then wipe dry with another clean cloth.

- Rub vinegar on the seals of the refrigerator to prevent mildew.

Tips for the Garage

- Wipe down a bicycle once a month with furniture polish to clean it and help prevent rust.

- Use tea to clean rusty garden tools. Brew a few pots of strong black tea. When cool, pour into a bucket. Soak the tools for a few hours, then wipe each one dry with a cloth. (Wear rubber gloves or your hands will be stained.)

- Holes in screens? Dab clear nail polish over each small hole.

- Stretch a rubber band around the rim of an open paint can, to wipe your brush on and keep paint off the side of the can.

- Use toothpaste to clear up hazy car headlights.

Tips on Odors

- Sprinkle laundry baskets and trash cans with baking soda.

- To remove odors from a microwave, fill a bowl with one cup of water and sprinkle your favorite spice, such as cinnamon, over it or add several drops of vanilla or lemon extract. Microwave on high for two to three minutes to bring it to a boil and let it sit inside for 10 to 15 minutes to cool before removing it. Wipe down the microwave's walls with paper towels or a clean sponge and leave the door open to air it out.

- Place an opened box of baking soda or a cup of ground coffee in your refrigerator or freezer to deodorize it.

- Insert a fabric softener sheet into smelly shoes or a smelly suitcase or gym bag. Prevent old books from smelling musty when in storage by putting a fabric softener sheet between two of the pages of each book.

Tips on Dust

- Give cloth or plastic lampshades a shower. Use your hand-held shower head, if you have one. Then leave the shades in the bathtub to dry. Do not use on silk or wood lampshades. You can also hold your hand inside the shade while you roll a lint roller over it.

- Place silk flowers in a bag with a cup of salt and shake to remove dust.

- Wipe electronics or dusty venetian blinds with a fabric softener sheet. It removes the dust, as well as the electrical charge that attracts dirt.

- Use hydrogen peroxide to clean and disinfect a keyboard. Dip a cotton swab in hydrogen peroxide to get into those nooks and crannies.

- Use white bread to dust an oil painting. Gently dab a slice of white bread over the surface to pick up dirt and grime.

- To clean a dirty stuffed animal, place it inside a lingerie bag and wash on the gentle cycle. The lingerie bag also provides protection during the drying process, so that the animal's eyes or nose do not disappear.

- Roll horizontal window blinds in the reverse direction, if you are concerned that they are dusty when unexpected guests arrive.

TIPS ON STAINS

- Fill the dishwasher's cleanser receptacle with white vinegar or lemon flavored Kool-Aid and run it through the dishwasher.

- Do not use your hand to brush away pollen from clothes or a tablecloth, because oil from your hand will set the stain. Use a piece of transparent tape to remove pollen from cloth. Rinse with cold water.

EMERGENCY STAIN REMOVAL TIPS

Stain	Solution	Notes
Blood	Hydrogen peroxide	Saturate the spot with hydrogen peroxide. Leave on for 30 minutes. If the spot remains, add more hydrogen peroxide and continue soaking.
Chocolate	Hydrogen peroxide	Scrape off the residue with a butter knife. Apply one tablespoon of hydrogen peroxide and rub with a wet toothbrush.
Coffee or tea	White vinegar	Saturate the area with a solution of one-half white vinegar and one-half cold water. Let sit for 30 minutes.
Crayon on a painted wall	WD-40	Spray some WD-40 on the pen, crayon, or scuff marks and wipe them away with a damp sponge.
Grass	Rubbing alcohol	Dab the marks with rubbing alcohol several times, using a cotton ball or sponge. If the stains persist, sponge with white vinegar.
Grease	Dish detergent WD-40	Rub dish detergent into the stain. Let sit for 30 minutes. Spray WD-40 on the stain and let sit for 30 minutes.
Gum	Ice cube and dish detergent	Rub an ice cube over the spot to freeze the gum. Chip away as much as possible with a butter knife. Dab dish detergent on any remaining residue.
Ink	Rubbing alcohol Milk Hand sanitizer gel	Dab the stain with rubbing alcohol several times, using a cotton ball or sponge. Saturate the spot with whole or low-fat milk. Let sit for two hours. Squirt the stain with the gel and let sit for 10 minutes.

E MERGENCY STAIN REMOVAL TIPS, CONTINUED...

Stain	Solution	Notes
Juice	Boiling water Ammonia	Stretch the stained area over a basin or bowl set in the sink. Carefully pour boiling water onto the spot. Dab the stain with an ammonia solution (one part ammonia to two parts water), using a cotton ball.
Lipstick and makeup	Hair spray	Saturate the spot with hair spray and let sit for 10 minutes.
Mud	Potato	Let the mud dry. Brush off what you can with an old toothbrush. Cut a potato in half and rub it over the stain for a few minutes. The enzymes in the potato help lift the stain out. Then machine wash.
Tomato sauce	Lemon juice	Scrape off residue with a spoon. Rinse with cold water. Sponge on one-quarter cup of lemon juice. Let sit for 10 minutes. Then machine wash.
Urine	White vinegar	Blot the wet area. Mix one or two cups of a solution of one-third white vinegar and two-thirds cool water, depending on size of stain. Pour the mixture on the stain and blot some more. Place a few layers of paper towels over the wet mark and step on them to absorb the liquid. Rinse with water until vinegar odor disappears and blot again. Use a fan or blow dryer to speed the drying.
Wine	Club soda	Blot (do not rub) stain with a paper towel. Dab club soda on the stain. Repeat the procedure as needed.

Chapter Eighteen
Conquering the Clutter

My dad never had a gray hair on his head to the day he died. When I asked him, "Are you dyeing your hair?" he would respond, "Of course not. I have just been blessed with youthful hair." For years, he defiantly denied the use of hair dye.

After my parents died, I cleaned out their house. For more than 30 years they lived there, and I do not think they ever threw out anything. The day I was cleaning out the linen closet, way back on one of the shelves behind the blankets, I reached in and to my surprise, there was a box of Grecian Formula Hair Dye. I looked up, smiled, and said, "Gotcha, Dad!"

Clutter is probably the most stressful word in my dictionary, and unfortunately I inherited the bad habit from my parents. I have lived in my home for more than 30 years—a home with two floors, plus an attic, basement, and two-car garage. There has been plenty of potential for amassing and storing a lot of things, and I have taken full advantage of that potential. But I have found that when I take the time to declutter a space, it has such an emotionally uplifting effect. I can go by that space and feel so much calmer than I was when I looked at the cluttered version.

Most women experience a significant boost in confidence and a reduction in stress levels after cleaning out a closet.

But, if you are like me, the clutter can be overwhelming. I think of all the areas I could work on, and that even after spending hours finishing that one area, it would only be like removing one seat from Fenway Park. But I have decided to do the following: Each week, on the day before the trash is picked up, I will take a large trash bag and fill it with things to throw out. Sometimes, if I am ambitious, I will fill two bags. I know it is not much, but at least I think that I am making some continual headway, and it does not take that much time or effort.

If you are like me, the clutter can be overwhelming.

Here are some other ideas that I have found helpful.

DONATE FOR A GOOD CAUSE—AND FOR YOUR SANITY

- **Clothing**, household goods, and accessories: The Salvation Army (www.salvationarmy.com), Goodwill (www.goodwill.org), and your local charities are always looking for them.

- **Books:** Reader to Reader (www.readertoreader.org) donates books to schools in need, including over 300,000 books sent to libraries in communities affected by Hurricane Katrina. Project Literacy (www.projectliteracy.com) sends books to schools, prisons, libraries, hospitals, and communities to promote literacy.

- **Eyeglasses:** Give the Gift of Sight (www.onesight.org) sends glasses to poor and developing countries. Drop-off points include LensCrafters, Pearle Vision, Sears Optical, Target Optical, and any Lions Club location.

- **Cell phones and rechargeable batteries:** Call2Recycle (www.call2recycle.org) collects and resells phones, with drop-off points that include Best Buy, Home Depot, Lowe's, and Staples. Cell Phones for Soldiers (www.cellphonesforsoldiers.com) provides cost-free communication services to active-duty military members and veterans.

- **Coats:** One Warm Coat (www.onewarmcoat.org) redistributes coats in the communities where they are originally donated.

- **Computer equipment:** The National Cristina Foundation (www.cristina.org) matches up the equipment you have with a local nonprofit, school, or public agency that is looking for that equipment. Once a match is made, the donor and recipient can arrange for a drop-off or pickup of the equipment. Other organizations include www.worldcomputerexchange.org, www.c4k.org, and www.computerswithcauses.org.

- **Musical instruments:** The organization Hungry for Music (www.hungryformusic.org) collects and provides used musical instruments to underprivileged students. If the instrument is particularly valuable, the organization will resell it, and the money will go toward the purchase of several instruments for kids in need.

- **Professional women's clothes:** Dress for Success (www.dressforsuccess.org) helps disadvantaged women around the world who are interviewing for jobs by giving them professional, gently worn outfits, shoes, and accessories.

- **Shoes:** Soles4Souls (www.soles4souls.org) distributes your old shoes to those in need in more than 120 countries. Nike

Reuse-A-Shoe (www.nike.com/grind) turns old sneakers into material for tennis and basketball courts and other surfaces.

- **Anything else:** Just about anything can be given away for free by visiting www.freecycle.org or www.freeuse.org. If you are not sure where you can donate items, you can also visit www.networkforgood.com, which will help you find the right fit.

GET INTO A ROUTINE

- Establish a routine and continue to take baby steps toward your goal. For example, spend 10 to 15 minutes per day or one hour on a particular day of the week to pick up in one room.

- Start small. Begin in the room where you spend your most time, so you can benefit most from your efforts. Or start with the bathroom, so you can practice on a smaller space.

- Tackle one area at a time and allow enough time to do it. Try not to get too frustrated. It is going to take some time to clear things up; after all, it took some time to accumulate them. Break it down into manageable chunks, such as the drawer full of photos or the chairs in the bedroom that have collected clothes.

- Set goals for rooms. Make a room-by-room list of what you want to accomplish in the next eight weeks. A list for your bathroom, for example, could include throwing out all expired medications and products. By jotting down goals for each room, you will alleviate some of the pressure of accomplishing the tasks all at once. Plus, you will have the satisfaction of checking off tasks as you complete them, which will provide you motivation to keep going.

- In a basket, place any items that do not belong in an area that you are working on. If your daughter's curling iron is on the kitchen table when you are cleaning the kitchen, set it in the basket and let her put it away in the right place.

- Place a dresser or storage unit near your home's entryway to store boots, shoes, gloves, and scarves.

PUT YOUR CLOSETS IN ORDER

- Use the shelf above the hanging bar in your closet for folded sweaters and boxed shoes. Use clear plastic boxes or label the boxes.

- Save the rack space in your closet by buying hangers that will accommodate multiple pairs of pants, shirts, and skirts. Or, use extension rods to make a second tier for hanging shorter items, such as shirts and pants.

- Put a clothes hamper in the bedroom closet to limit dirty clothes being dropped on the floor.

- Install hooks on the back of the door of the closet to hang items, such as belts, purses, ties, and scarves.

- Every time you take a hanging item out of the closet, take out the hanger, too, and keep it on the closet door handle. This makes it easier to hang the garment back up when you are done with it.

- Try the "One in, one out" rule to avoid building clutter. When you buy something new, choose something you own and put in a bag to give away.

- Establish some rules about your clothing ahead of time. For example, if you are not sentimental about a garment and you have not used it in two years or longer, get rid of it.

<u>STEPS TO SORTING YOUR CLOTHES:</u>

1. Remove about a quarter of your clothes from your closet. Most organizational experts recommend removing everything from the closet at once, but I think that generates too much pressure to organize it all at once.
2. Create four piles: clothes you like and wear regularly; clothes you might wear if you could make them work; clothes to donate; and clothes to throw away.
3. Anything with stains or rips should go into the throwaway pile.
4. Anything that does not fit, does not look good, or is uncomfortable should go into the donate pile.
5. If there is something that you want to keep for sentimental reasons, put it in a specially marked box and place it in the attic. Or take a photo of it and donate it or throw it out.
6. Avoid the "Maybe I should keep it, because it will come back into style" syndrome. The truth is that most fads return, but usually with new variations. You probably will have to repurchase it when the time comes anyway.
7. Avoid the "Maybe I will lose weight and be able to wear it again" syndrome. This syndrome not only keeps

your closet cluttered and causing you stress, but every time you see the item, you are sent a negative message, reminding you that you have not lost the weight. When (not if) you do lose the weight, treat yourself to a new outfit.

8. When done, make a list of items you need to buy to make new outfits out of the clothes you already own.

9. Put the clothes back into the closet, organized in any way that makes sense to you–warm weather versus cold weather, tops versus bottoms, casual versus work versus dressy.

Seek professional help when all else fails. The nonprofit National Association of Professional Organizers (NAPO) lists members specializing in residential organization at www.napo.net.

Savor the Victory

G iven the early deaths of my father, mother, and sister, I always had the goal to retire at the age of 55. That nicely corresponded with when our younger son would graduate from college and tuition payments would end. I ended up retiring 18 months earlier than my original plan.

I loved working at Phillips Academy up until the last 15 months. That is when, for the first time in my career, I was directly confronted with a female bully. I had been instrumental in hiring her into an entry level position, and supported her as she advanced within the business and human resources departments. However, once promoted into a management position, she made it difficult for me, members of my department, and many other talented Phillips Academy colleagues. The collaborative, constructive, and collegial environment to which I was always accustomed was no longer present. For more than a year, I and numerous others brought the problem to her manager's attention. But he did not have the strength nor experience to confront conflict, so the difficult working environment continued, and I found that needless tension in the workplace was negatively affecting my health.

Fortunately, I was in a financial position in which I had the freedom to choose what I wanted to do. I chose to retire. It was one of the hardest professional decisions I have ever made, but the right one.

When I retired from Phillips Academy, it was the first time in my adult life that I was not working full time professionally. The transition from a longtime, full-time professional working mother to a retired empty nester was not easy. During the first three months of retirement, I enjoyed the peaceful quiet of my local library and read just about every "How to make the most out of retirement" book that the library had on its shelves. I joined a health club and began the process of improving myself both physically and emotionally. Six months later, I became a volunteer for the Big Brothers Big Sisters organization. I also decided to do some freelance technology and management consulting, and to hold leadership volunteer roles in political campaigns. I continue to keep busy doing the things I want to do, not what I have to do.

In August 2011, Tony and I attended his 40th high school reunion in Mayfield, Pennsylvania, a small town about 10 miles from Scranton. We met up with two of the ushers from our wedding, Pete and Gary, and their wives, Jane and Pat, respectively. We had not seen one another for more than 25 years, but had such a wonderful, relaxed evening. Jane said, "We should all plan a vacation together some time. It would be fun."

Immediately, Gary, a prominent pathologist in northeastern Pennsylvania, responded, "Where do we want to go? Anyone interested in Hawaii? I have a friend who has a three-bedroom condo on the beach on the southwest side of Oahu that we can get for free."

We were flabbergasted, rendered speechless for a few moments, and then simultaneously responded, "Are you kidding?"

We agreed on dates that worked for all of us, and Gary said he would check with his friend to see if those dates worked for him. To be honest, we never thought we would hear about it again. But four months later, Gary informed us that we were off to Hawaii.

We could not believe it, and when we arrived at the condo, we were even more stunned. It was right on the beach, with private lagoons, pools, and beautiful landscaping, yet only a 20-minute drive from the hustle and bustle of Honolulu.

I had been a bit nervous about the trip. Tony was with his longtime childhood friends. I had only seen Jane and Pat a couple of times in my life. Would it be awkward spending seven days in a condo together? Interestingly enough, not only was the company of Jane and Pat fun and enjoyable, it was very enlightening.

Jane was still working professionally, holding a stressful executive position, and counting the days to retirement. She was checking emails and never totally disconnected from work. Pat had been a nurse for many years and stopped working professionally once she had her first child. She was reading, staying in contact with family, and studying for a class she was taking at a local college. We talked about our life phases. Right there before my eyes was one woman who I had been like two years earlier, and the other woman who I wanted to be like two years into the future.

One early Saturday morning in July 2013, I woke up and signed into Facebook. There was a private message from my college friend, Cindy, about her husband of 32 years. It read, "Hi Val, I want to let you know of our terrible tragedy. While Tom was riding his bike on Wednesday, he was hit by a dump truck and killed instantly. We're grateful that he didn't suffer. The boys and I are doing ok, processing it a little at a time. The funeral is Monday morning."

I sat there in shock, not knowing how to react. I had just seen Cindy at our Wellesley College reunion, where we had talked about our families and reminisced about the great times we had together. Tears rolled down my cheeks. I had to respond, but what could I say? After five minutes, I wrote a reply. I told her how sorry I was and assured her that my love, my prayers, and my thoughts were with her and her family.

After an hour of sitting motionless on the couch, I made reservations for the plane, the hotel, and the rental car to visit her in Baltimore. I was finally together enough to pick up the phone and call her. I told her my plans and set off for one of the saddest journeys of my life.

I spent the next few days with Cindy and her family. I had not seen many of them for years, so it was comforting to see them and talk to them. I was reminded of how our time on this earth can end at any moment. I had been striving to live each day doing the things I loved since my retirement, and I loved this phase of my life. After so many years of struggling to schedule so many activities for my career and my family, I was embracing the wiggle room that retirement brought to my crowded hours. I was delighted to be there for Cindy, and for myself, sharing the sadness, and welcoming the support of old friends in the inevitable crises that crash into our lives.

"That damn Donna Reed"

A few years ago, I was watching an episode of *The Gilmore Girls* entitled "That Damn Donna Reed." A young man in the episode asked, "Who is Donna Reed?"

The collective response from his girlfriend and her mother was, "The quintessential 1950s mom with the perfect 1950s family; never without a smile and high heels; with hair that would crack if you hit it with a hammer."

The young man queried, "So it's a show?"

To which they responded, "It's a lifestyle. It's a religion."

Later in the episode, when the young man's girlfriend tried to be like Donna Reed to please him, he said, "I don't expect you to be Donna Reed. I don't want you to be Donna Reed. I'm happy with you."

I thought of my mother, and how I wished she could have seen that episode. We all just need to learn to be happy with ourselves.

I have been thinking about writing this book ever since my mother died. I have never written and published a book before, and wondered whether I could accomplish such an ambitious goal. What I did learn was that the journey, daunting at times, was well worth the effort.

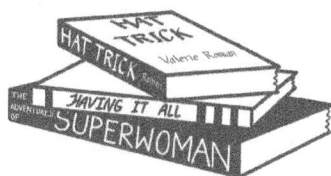

My first draft was very impersonal. It provided "the facts, just the facts," bullet after bullet of ideas that I had gathered in the hatbox. I was afraid to reveal myself. After all, who was I to think that others might be interested in my life? It was my son, Matthew, who encouraged me to include my own experiences in this book, and I am so happy that he gave me that advice. The process allowed me to remember so many of the good times in my life, as well as some of the painful memories. It allowed me to analyze what I thought worked and what I thought did not work out so well; what I would do moving forward and what I would not do; what was important to me and what was not.

The game is over now, the buzzer has sounded, and I have

scored my hat trick. I hope you will join me in pursuing your own life goals, rather than a cookie-cutter ideal that society has created. You are the best one to live the life that you have been given.

Throughout my life, I have played numerous roles as a daughter, a sister, a colleague, a wife, a mother, a boss, and a friend. I have developed positive, fulfilling, and rewarding personal relationships. I am proud of who I have become and I know that my parents would be proud of me. You, too, should be proud of who you are.

Embrace your flaws – we all have them – but focus on your strengths. That is the key to scoring a hat trick in life. Focusing on your strengths will enable you to fulfill your unique potential.

Acknowledgements

After thirty years of research and ten years of writing, I am so grateful to the many people who supported me throughout the development of this book.

First, I want to lovingly acknowledge my husband, Tony, and sons, Matthew and David, for their patience, advice, and unwavering support. I want to thank my sister-in-law, Judie Roman and my high school teacher, Sheila Segal, for their inspiration, helpful suggestions, and continued encouragement. I also want to thank Kathryn Kretschmer-Weyland, Britt Edwards, and Chris Aguilar, for their friendship, advice, and assistance, and to Maggie Marquis for posing for the photograph on the book's cover.

I am also grateful to the wonderful professionals with whom I had the opportunity to work. I thank Sarah Dautel and Claire McCrea for their professionalism, keen eye, and editing expertise. I thank Hannah Dautel for her talent and art work that brought life to these pages. I am grateful to Holly Harper for her design magic and vision. And last, but certainly not least, I want to thank Ellen E.M. Roberts for bringing her years of experience assisting authors to this project.

Resources

www.umassmed.edu/cfm/
The UMass Medical School Center for Mindfulness provides education, mindfulness-based stress reduction (MBSR) programs, and other tools to improve well-being and realize human potential.

www.mindbodygreen.com
MindBodyGreen (MBG) brings together leaders and experts in the wellness world to provide the freshest, most in-the-know content and tools to help live the healthiest, happiest life.

www.success.com
SUCCESS is a newsstand publication and website that serves as a guide for personal and professional development through inspiration, motivation, and training.

www.healthywomen.org
HealthyWomen's award-winning website was one of the first sites dedicated solely to women's health and is recognized nationally as a go-to source for trustworthy health information for women. This resource gives women the latest health information, including news updates, health tips, resources, and extensive coverage of hundreds of health topics.

www.drnorthrup.com
Christine Northrup, M.D. author of Women's Bodies, Women's Wisdom provides the most up-to-date information available on the entire range of women's health concerns, including nutrition, breast health, fertility, menopause, dozens of new natural treatments, and a wealth of hard-to-find health care resources.

GOAL TWO: **HAVE A GREAT CAREER**

www.catalyst.org
Founded in 1962, Catalyst is a nonprofit organization and resource for research, information, and advice about women at work. It brings together experts from around the world to share knowledge and shape the dialogue about inclusive leadership and other critical factors related to women and workplaces around the globe.

www.ellevatenetwork.com
Ellevate Network is a community of professional women who care about investing in themselves and in other women. Its mission is to help women advance in the workplace, both for themselves and the greater good.

www.passthetorchforwomen.org

Pass The Torch for Women is a community that guides women as they navigate their career pathways by providing mentoring and networking opportunities.

www.livecareer.com/quintessential

Quintessential Careers is a one-stop source for the latest career tools, job search tips, and expert advice. No matter where you are in your career, it can help empower you to find the success you deserve.

www.nafe.com

The National Association for Female Executives, one of the country's largest associations for women professionals and business owners, offers education, resources, skills development, and networking to professional women to achieve career success.

GOAL THREE: RAISE A HAPPY FAMILY

www.workingmomsagainstguilt.com

Working Moms Against Guilt is an online community that serves as an outlet and resource for moms all over the world who battle guilt at the office, at family functions, in the minivan, on the playground—you name it. It aims to help women win the battle and feel good (or at least, good enough) about themselves, their choices, and their lives.

www.workingmother.com

Working Mother supports the country's more than 17 million moms devoted to their families and committed to their careers. Through its website and magazine, it provides working mothers the community, solutions, and strategies needed to thrive.

www.wix.com/workingmothers/org

The National Association of Working Mothers helps mothers balance personal well-being, family life , and work, while improving their lifestyles, through resources, education, and Information.

www.simplifymagazine.com

Simplify Magazine is a quarterly, digital publication that pulls together experts in various fields to address some of the most pressing needs of the modern family.

www.realsimple.com

Real Simple offers realistic solutions, cleaning tricks, time-saving tips, etiquette musts, and more simple solutions for everyday life.

Bombeck, Erma. *Motherhood, The Second Oldest Profession.* New York: McGraw-Hill, 1983

Collins, Gail. *When Everything Changed: The Amazing Journey of American Women from 1960 to the Present.* New York: Little, Brown and Company, 2009

Ephron, Nora. *The Most of Nora Ephron.* New York: Knopf, 2013

Fey, Tina. *Bossypants.* New York: Little, Brown and Company, 2011

Gilbert, Elizabeth. *Eat, Pray, Love.* New York: Penguin Books, 2007

Irving, John. *The World According to Garp.* New York: Ballantine Books, 1990

Kay, Katty, and Claire Shipman. *The Confidence Code.* New York: HarperBusiness, 2014

Quindlen, Anna. *Lots of Candles, Plenty of Cake.* New York: Random House, 2013

Rayburn, Carole and Lillian Comas-Diaz. *WomanSoul: The Inner Life of Women's Spirituality.* Westport, CT: Praeger Publishers, 2008

Steinem, Gloria. *Revolution From Within.* New York: Little, Brown and Company, 1993

Index

A

acids 49, 59, 82, 88-89
    amino 26, 40, 88-89
    ellagic 47, 57
    fatty 49, 59, 82, 88
    folic 82, 88
    malic 46
adrenalin (see: neurotransmitters)
acupressure 60, 62, 65-66, 135
Albright, Madeleine 15, 106
alcohol 23, 27, 69
alertness 40, 62, 82, 89, 137
Alba, Jessica 3
Allen, David 153
Alzheimer's Disease 139
Andover (see: Phillips Academy)
antidepressants 22, 32, 88
antioxidants 58-59, 63, 68, 82, 88
aromatherapy and essential oils 70-71, 137-139
asthma 57-58, 138-139
attitude management 82, 112, 121
    forgiveness 93, 133
    gratitude 90-91, 166, 174, 192, 230
    insecurity 117

B

Beeton, Isabella 6
Bergen, Candace 3
Blau, Ludwig W. 64
blood pressure 21, 58-59, 63, 73, 129
blood sugar 26, 34, 43, 137
Bombeck, Erma 94, 237
Bowdoin College 95
bread 25, 62, 209, 215
Bullock, Sandra 3
Burns, David 87
Byrne, Rhonda 87

C

caffeine 43, 59-60, 69
Cambridge, City of 100, 103-104, 108, 124
cancer 21, 31, 33, 35, 47, 57-58, 63-64, 94
capsaicin 26
carbohydrates 26-27, 41-42, 62, 72, 88
career 2-3, 99-101, 117-118, 123-127, 235-236
    bullying 106
    hiring people 112-113
    ladder 118
    managing people 110-112
    mentoring 100, 105, 110, 126, 236
    networking 122-124, 236
    working with women 103-119, 227

Carroll, Diahann 2
Carter, Jimmy 103
Catalyst 124, 235
Census Bureau 99-100, 103, 105, 121, 126, 159, 169
cereal 26, 62
Chin Lui, Helen 66
chocolate 59-60, 63, 137, 216
cholesterol 21, 24, 59, 62-63, 73
Clinton, Hillary 15, 87, 106, 161-162
clothing and accessories 50-53
closet organization 223-225
color selection 50-52, 116
coffee 39, 58, 60, 63, 65, 81, 210, 214, 216
colds and flu 60
Colette, Sidonie-Gabrielle 91
communication, effective 112-116, 122
commuting 35, 142
congestion 60-61
Conran, Shirley 6
cookie swaps 205-207, 210
cooking 205, 208-210
cough remedies 60, 67, 139, 201
curcumin 68

D

dairy 23-24, 29, 41, 72-74, 180
Dalai Lama 90
Dartmouth College 95
day care 142, 198-200
DeFrain, Andrea Mutch 19
dementia 64, 81
depression 31, 62, 87-88, 90, 93, 129, 139
diuretics 25, 69
downsizing and donations 220-222

E

ears, earlobes 66, 135, 201
eggs 22, 24, 72-73, 209
elderberry 60
email 116, 145, 148, 153-154
emergencies 52, 71
Emmons, Robert 90
energy 26, 30, 34, 39-43, 72-73, 88-90, 137
Epictetus 95
eucalyptus 30, 139
evil eye 165
exercise 21, 24, 30-37, 58, 69, 81, 90, 92, 133, 135
    stretching 34-36, 42, 69, 93, 117, 135
    Tai Chi 56
    yoga 36
eyes 46, 72, 116, 119

F

Facebook 3, 118, 122-123, 229
family
    sit-down dinners 208-209
    traditions 176, 196-198
    vacations 134, 179, 194
fatigue 40-41, 62, 137, 139
fats 24-27, 41-42
Fenway Park 16, 39, 220
fiber 24, 57, 59, 62
flavonoids 59, 68
flaxseed 59, 63, 73
Fonda, Jane 3, 32
fruit 22-23, 28-29, 40-41, 62
    apples 58, 72
    avocados 25, 40, 63, 72-74
    bananas 25, 40-41, 61, 72-74
    berries 46-47, 57-58, 63-64, 72, 82, 88
    cherries 64
    citrus fruit 72, 82
    dried fruit 41-42, 73
    grapefruits 26, 57, 139
    grapes 25
    kiwifruit 72
    lemons 26, 48, 68, 138-139, 209,
        214-215, 217
    mangoes 40, 72-73
    melons 26, 64, 69, 72-74
    oranges 26, 40, 64, 72, 139
    prunes and raisins 72-73
    tangerines 72
    tomatoes 25-26, 40, 48, 72, 74, 217

G

gall bladder 21
gender equality 193
Greek culture
    food 19-21
    heritage 12, 15-17, 45-46, 159-160, 162,
        165, 196
    travel 32, 85-87
gum 26, 82, 216

H

hair care 47, 116
Hamm, Mia 3
happiness 87-95, 134, 139, 143, 231
headaches 63, 66-67, 139
heartburn 62
heart health 21, 33, 41, 57, 59, 63, 66-67, 70, 72,
    87, 129
Hepburn, Audrey 2
herbs 62, 67-69, 82

chamomile 139
gingko biloba 82
Heslin, Cindy Romer 18, 230
Holmes-Rahe stress scale 140
hormones 31, 75, 83, 89-90, 139
    cortisol 83
    endorphins 31, 88-89
    estrogen 57, 89
humor 94, 108-109, 136, 172

I

infection 65-66, 139, 201-202
infertility 21, 129, 164
inflammation 47-48, 64, 67, 75
insect and mosquito bites 64, 70-71

J

Jefferson, Thomas 92
journals 28, 90, 137
Jung, Carl 136

K

Kelly, Grace 2
Kennedy, John F. 99
kidneys 55, 63
Klein, Gail Printy 91, 105

L

Labo, Melinda Ouellette 91, 199
LaLanne, Jack 32
lavender 70-71, 139
Lever, Janet 107
life balance pie chart 131
lycopene 48, 57

M

massage 47-49, 53, 60, 89, 135, 141, 175
McLean, Taryn 194
meats 22-23, 67, 72-74
    beef 72, 74
    chicken 23, 40-41, 61, 72-73
    poultry 22, 72-74
    turkey 40, 72
meditation 92, 133-134
meetings and agendas 51, 109, 111, 114-115, 127,
    143
melatonin 89
memory 62, 68, 73, 75, 77-83, 88, 139
metabolism 25-26, 28, 72-73

migraines (see: headaches)
minerals 69-70, 73-74
  calcium 27, 41, 69-70, 72-73
  carotene 73
  echinacea 60
  folate 70
  magnesium 41, 60, 69, 73, 75
  omega 59, 73, 82, 88
  potassium 41, 74
  selenium 74
  thiamine 71-72
  zinc 60, 74
mint 62, 70-71, 82, 137, 139
mood management 42, 88-90, 137, 139
Moore, Mary Tyler 3
Morter, M. T. 92
Munsey, Bob 105, 126

N

nail care 46-47
nausea 62, 67
neurotransmitters 40, 42, 88-89, 136
Nooyi, Indra 3
nuts 25, 41, 57-59, 73-75
  almonds 40, 59, 82
  brazil nuts 58, 74
  cashews 25, 73
  peanuts 40-41, 59, 70, 72-73
  pecans 63
  walnuts 25, 59, 63, 73, 82

O

oatmeal 23, 41, 64, 72
Obama, Michelle 3
odors 213-214
oils 23, 25, 60, 62, 70-72
  canola 23, 25
  citronella 70
  fish 137
  hydrogenated oil 24, 60
  olive 23, 25, 45-46, 49, 53, 58, 64
organization tips 151-155, 179-185, 202-203,
  224-225
digital files 154
  email 153-154
  folders 118, 144, 152-154, 180
  paper management 144, 151-152, 180
  storage control 182-183, 214, 223

P

pain 64-67, 69, 75, 135, 139, 165-167, 206, 231
peppermint 62, 70-71, 137, 139

perfectionism 2-4, 13, 15, 140, 149, 160-161, 177,
  190, 207, 231
peroxide 47, 214, 216
Phillips, Kathie 91
Phillips Academy 100, 103, 105, 125-126, 227-
  228
pregnancy 104, 140, 163-167
premenstrual syndrome 69
professional development 103, 105, 110, 116, 122
protein 22-24, 28, 41-42, 59, 65, 72, 88

R

Reagan, Ronald 103
Reed, Donna 2, 13-15, 160-162, 207, 230-231
reflexology (see: acupressure)
relaxation 35-36, 89, 134-139, 175
retirement 5, 227-230
rice 61-62, 72
Roberts, Cokie 15
Rodin, Judith 6
Roosevelt, Eleanor 95
Ross, Julia 88

S

sandalwood 139
Sandberg, Sheryl 3, 118, 124
Sawyer, Diane 15
seafood 22, 40, 58, 72-74, 82
  oysters 72, 74
  salmon 25, 59, 72-73
  swordfish 72
  tuna 41, 72-73
Sedaris, David 94
seeds 40, 67
  pumpkin 40, 69, 72-73
  sunflower 25, 70, 75
Segal, Sheila 16, 92, 105
serotonin (see: neurotransmitters)
Shimoff, Marci 87
Simmons College 16
simplify your life 147-148, 179
  helpful technologies 145-147, 153-155
skin care 47-49, 58, 63-64, 71, 116, 139
  acne 48, 65
  exfoliation 49
  facial 48, 89
  pimples 45, 48
  retinol 48
sleep, problems 21, 35, 89, 139
sleep, value of 30, 82, 137, 200
snacks 24, 29, 41-43, 59, 88
soda 27, 57, 213-214, 217
sodium 23, 27, 65, 74
Somersworth, NH 3, 11, 16, 45, 160
sore throat 61, 66

soup 23, 26, 42, 57, 61, 68
soy 24-25, 40, 57, 59, 72-74
spa 141, 147
spices 67-68, 214
    basil 67, 139
    cinnamon 26, 69, 75, 214
    cloves 63, 65, 67
    cumin 67
    fennel 68
    garlic 61
    ginger 62, 67, 137, 139
    pepper 25-26, 139, 202
    rosemary 139
    sage 139
    turmeric 58, 68
sports 1-3, 6, 32-33, 37, 104, 107, 125-126, 142,
    173-174, 194, 196, 203
    baseball 33, 40, 107, 194
    basketball 36, 106-107, 126, 173, 194, 222
    football 33, 104, 107, 126, 173, 194
    hockey 2, 174, 194
    horseback riding 174
    soccer 3, 32, 36, 101, 107, 194, 199
stains 46-47, 213, 215-217, 224
Steinbrenner, George 170
Stewart, Martha 6
stomach
    cancer 58
    digestion 27, 41, 61-62, 66
    exercises 35-36
    fat 24, 26, 63, 83
    problems and pain 62-63, 66, 68, 139
Stott, Susan 126
Streep, Meryl 3
stress 75, 83, 89-90, 95, 118, 129-140
stroke 21, 63-64, 67, 129
sugar 23-27, 41, 57, 63, 209
sunlight 42, 48, 63, 72
sunscreen 47-48

T

tea 29, 42, 48, 58, 62, 67, 137, 213, 216
thyroid 63, 163-164
Tibet 134
tickler file 151-152, 179-180
Title IX U.S. Education Amendments 107
Tolle, Eckhart 87
Tooth care 30, 46-47, 61, 65, 67, 201
tyrosine 40, 89

V

vegetables 22-23, 28-29, 40, 57, 62, 68-69
    asparagus 69, 72-73
    broccoli 57, 64, 72-73
    brussels spouts 72

cabbage 57, 72
carrots 40, 63, 72-73, 137
cauliflower 57, 72
celery 59, 69
cucumbers 63
edamame 70
green leafy 22, 70, 73, 75, 82
legumes 42, 72-74
lentils 22, 62, 73
mushrooms 72-74
olives 25, 63
onions 69
peppers 26, 64, 72
potatoes 25-26, 62, 72-74, 137
salad 42, 67-68
spinach 72-74
squash 26, 73
vinegar 21, 47-48, 212-213, 215-217
vitamins 69-70, 72
    multivitamin 23
    vitamin A 72
    vitamin B 41, 71-72, 82, 88
    vitamin C 25, 41, 64, 72, 75, 82
    vitamin D 63, 70, 72
    vitamin E 69, 72, 82
    vitamin K 72

W

water 27, 42-43, 48, 61, 65, 69
Weaver, Sigourney 3
weight management 19-30
Weight Watchers 22
Weil, Andrew 133
Wellesley College 3, 15-16, 18-19, 32, 39-40, 99-
    100, 106, 121, 126, 193, 208
wheat germ 72-74
Whitman, Meg 3
whole grains 22, 28, 41, 62, 72-74
Windham, NH 160, 205
wine 27, 61, 181, 217
working with women (see career)
Wurtman, Judith 88

Y

yogurt 23, 25, 40-41, 63, 74
YouTube 94, 133, 136

Z

Zuckerberg, Mark 118

About the Author

After graduating from Wellesley College, Valerie Roman worked full time in the technology management field for more than 30 years. She was the first Chief of Systems Analysis and Design for the Census Bureau in Washington, D.C., was the first technology director for the City of Cambridge, Massachusetts, and was the director of technology for Phillips Academy in Andover, Massachusetts. She continues to consult for municipalities and schools throughout New England. Her passions include sports—as a lifelong fan of all Boston teams—and politics. She is married and a mother of two, and lives in New Hampshire.

Valerie Roman became aware at an early age that many women feel they need to live up to some ideal - whether it's the model on the magazine cover, the neighbor who founded a multi-million dollar business, or the perfect mother on a television show. In Hat Trick, she provides women the motivation and advice to fight that battle. Valerie Roman offers a toolbox of techniques for everything from cultivating healthy habits to organizing closets; from running a meeting to raising ethical kids; from simplifying life with technology to working with other women. In a fun and fact-filled playbook about juggling family, career, and personal well-being, Valerie Roman shares her decades of experience and her lifelong library of advice culled from magazines, books, the Internet, and television to help a new generation of women be all that they can be.

www.ingramcontent.com/pod-product-compliance
Lightning Source LLC
Chambersburg PA
CBHW021222090426

42740CB00006B/328